FORCED PATHS

ORDERED STEPS

When Our Addiction Meets Jesus

David

Psalm 19: 14

Jemal Damtawe

October 17, 2020

JEMAL DAMTAWE

DEDICATION

I dedicate this memoir to all who still suffer, to those who recovered from their inner conflicts, addiction and severe trauma. To the many that have lost loved ones, I trust that you may find peace and hope. For those who still suffer, I pray you will seek His unconditional love, mercy and grace. To my cherished friends, I thank you for your trust and compassion. To my wife, I say, "My love for you shall live forever in my heart. You are the best possible dream come true, and I thank you for your boundless acceptance and love." May God welcome this dedication as an offering, revealing His healing power and eternal glory.

All Bible scriptures from New Kings James version.

CONTENTS

BIBLIOGRAPHY

Born and raised in Ethiopia, Jemal now resides on the west coast of Canada, in Coquitlam, British Columbia. He lives with his wife Vincia, and son Adam in a modest suburb home.

On December 28 -2005, Jemal entered the Union Gospel Mission drug and alcohol treatment program, commencing in March 2006. After working at UGM for many months doing maintenance work and at the thrift store, he began working as an outreach worker in Vancouver's downtown East Side.

Jemal was ordained as a Reverend in Alberta on June 2 - 2011. He ministers today, performing marriages, preaching and reaching out to the homeless and those who still suffer from addictions.

Today, Jemal travels around the lower mainland using UGM's Mobile Mission Rescue vehicle, connecting with the homeless and others less fortunate. It is a labour of love, giving back to the community.

Jemal's future hopes and plans look forward to opening a recovery home near where he lives in Coquitlam, named, Fork in the Road; a vision of helping all who struggle with their addictions.

PROLOGUE

I have lived a relatively active life. I've travelled the world and been placed in some unusual situations over the years. I thought that I had my fair share of stories to tell of being placed in "tight spots" and facing "challenging moments," stories I could pull out and share in the course of a conversation.

Then I met Jemal... His life has been a series of "tight spots" and "challenging moments" that are beyond what most of us could ever imagine. But it's not so much what happened "to" him that makes Jemal's life stand out. It is what happened "in" him...

It's been said that, "wisdom does not come from the circumstances in your life, wisdom comes from how you ultimately respond to the circumstances in your life." If that is true, you are about to read the story of a very wise man.

Over the years, I have watched Jemal transition from a single man to a married man. I have watched him transform into a loving husband and then doting father. I have watched him live out a calling to reach men and women who find themselves at the very bottom of the social ladder: men and women who are stuck; men and women who wander the streets of our city. I used to wonder what fueled Jemal's drive to head into that battleground - day after day, night after night. After reading his story, I no longer wonder. - Darin Latham, Lead Pastor, Broadway Church, Vancouver, B.C.

ACKNOLWLEGEMENTS

To God, I thank you for unfailing love and grace. As I arrive here at this book's fruition, I will never forget where the journey began. My heart cries with endless praise for your faithfulness, love and glory.

I thank my most precious wife, Vincia Damtawe. I thank you for the past nine years we have been together. I thank you for being who you are. Day after day, you stood faithfully by my side. Loving, encouraging, and challenging me. Thank you for your prayers, without you I could not have written this book.

Thank you to my daughter for her forgiveness and for giving our relationship a second chance.

Pastor Darin Latham; words are not enough to describe how deeply I appreciate you. I will cherish forever you helping me "practice the presence."

William Alex Watts; your story in this book will help many understand and feel what trauma can do. Also, your contribution shows how one can overcome and be set free. Thank you, my friend.

Kumar Sundarempilal; my counsellor and dear friend, you are the best. You helped save my life, and continue today as one I confide in and pray with.

David E Love; thank you for transcribing audio interviews, consultation, and crucial participation in writing, publishing my book. May we continue to pray with, and for each other.

To my best friend, Fari Gheam-Maghami; thank you for showing me what true friendship is all about. You walk what you preach and expect of others. You have been with me through good times and bad, and I thank you for that. The type of friend you are is hard to find, and I thank you for living your life this way.

Thank you Joanne Anderson: For who you are and praying for me. You are a true prayer warrior, and I appreciate what you did in my life. God bless you. I take this time to honour your mom and her memory.

Pastor Curt Bruneski; thank you for welcoming my family and I to Blue Mountain church with open arms. I appreciate everything you have done and your encouragement in my life. I appreciate your prayers and ask you never to stop praying for me. You have been by my side as a mentor and friend. I thank God for making our paths cross.

Peter Steffens; thank you for being a good friend, and for your support and encouragement. I appreciate our friendship and enjoy the time we spend together.

Rob Thompson; thank you for being who you; for the living words that you speak into my life. Thank you for support and prayer.

Matt Hislop; thank you for being a good friend, like a brother. You were there to support my recovery in the crucial stage; for believing in me.

UGM staff and Alumni; thank you for all that you have done in my life. You were the hands and feet of Jesus when I was walking in darkness. Thank you for your obedience to him because I would not have made it if it was not for you. The alumni brotherhood is dear to me, and we must continue to support and encourage each other each day. I am blessed to walk my life with you.

Thank you Jeremy Hunka; for inspiring me to take my story to the next level. You believed in me, and we all need people like you in our lives to cheer us on.

Pastor Rene Gallegos; Thank you for being one of the first to encourage me to read God's word and to pray. I know you have been praying for me in my life, and I thank you for that, my brother.

Mike Jobin and Johnny Ricci; thank you both for being there from the start of my journey at UGM. You each taught me a lot, supporting in the early part of my recovery. Even today, you continue to be good friends.

Jack Summerfield; thank you for supporting me in the early stages of my recovery, surrounding me with prayer and always showing concern for me.

To the memory of my mother Emit. The love of a mother is powerful. You are forever in my heart, and your love for me enabled me to fight for my life.

To the Damtawe family: I thank you all for your encouragement. I use the wonderful memories of the good times we had to get through my difficult life at times. I am blessed to have each of you and love being part of this family. Life tried to tear us apart, but our bond was too strong.

Melissa Crump: Thank you for always being there to watch Adam. It is greatly appreciated to have someone like you in our life. You are a wonderful aunt, and I am thankful for all the times you have helped Vincia and me.

Thank you, Denise Clare, for allowing my wife and I to attend our marriage retreat. You are truly selfless in your love for your family.

Jeremiah Touchbourne: Thank you, Jeremiah, for your friendship. It is a blessing to have known you all these years.

"Iron sharpeneth iron; so a man sharpeneth the countenance of his friend" - Proverbs 27:17.

INTRODUCTION

"The steps of a good man are ordered by the Lord. And he delights in his ways." Psalm 37:23 (NKJV)

This book is a memoir of specific life events, which Jemal relives with emotion and truth. He truly believes and lives by these words, "Our steps are ordered by the Lord." these words bring a wave of peace to many men. But for many years, he did not know a life of peace. Taken by force as a young boy and thrown into a life of violence and fighting in the Ethiopian civil war took a devastating toll. Finally escaping by hiding on a cargo ship, he left Ethiopia only to have the war follow him in the form of horrific memories. Alcohol, drugs, gangs, anger, and money would not let him forget what he saw and endured as a young man.

He fought sleepless nights with alcohol and the death of friends who used hard drugs. Although surrounded by people at times, he carried a heavy load of guilt, shame, and loneliness. Jemal was dealt a hard hand for much of his life and then found himself homeless, alone and hopeless.

Finding himself at a fork in the road, he journeyed down the difficult path of recovery, one day at a time until he had a spiritual awakening. John 8:13, "The Pharisees therefore said to Him, "You bear witness of Yourself; Your witness is not true."

When God frees you, you are free indeed. He found that this truly is correct. Once lost, his life is now a complete opposite of the one he was forced to live. He does not look back with shame now at the road he was forced to take but uses those memories to stay humble. Jemal can relate well to others who struggled with what he did. He feels their pain, trauma, and fear, their inner feelings of despair that only God can heal.

He uses his past to help others with addiction break free and live in peace. In this memoir, he is honest about all of his previous life and about how hard it was to move forward from suffering to the freedom. He encourages others to seek help, and allow Jesus to guide them out of the endless pit of addiction and sorrow.

There are so many wolves in sheep's clothing in life, but only Jesus is the true shepherd who will order and guide your steps. Jemal stands in awe as Jesus has restored his life and given him back what the locusts have stolen. He now identifies with father, husband, and Reverend but mostly as a forgiven child of God. We would all identify ourselves as forgiven when we give our shame and addictions to over to our Saviour. – Vincia Damtawe

Chapter 1

Kidnapped and Betrayed

As a young boy, I often dreamed of being a professional soccer player or movie star, but at the age of fifteen, my hopes faded away into a haze of confusion. Whilst walking to school, a van pulled alongside me and five uniformed soldiers jumped out, blasting their guns in the air. I saw a young teenager, about the same age as me massacred right in front of me as he tried to run. I saw his motionless body lying on the ground, covered in blood.

I saw bullets smashing into bodies, tearing off chunks of flesh ... blood is dripping from bodies. I closed my eyes and cried ... vomit churned in my throat as I trembled from the terror. We were just boys, carrying our books on the way to school when all this chaos surrounded us. Who wouldn't cry?

"Get in the truck or be killed," a soldier screamed at me. My mind locked in a terrifying 'fight or flight' mode. It all happened so fast, but I dared not defy his authority ... I wanted to live. It was like watching a horror movie with actors running around, screaming out of character, and not knowing what the next act would be.

The soldiers didn't want the girls that were walking alongside us. They were free to carry on down the road. I looked back and saw them crying, in shock as we drove away.

There was already a group of boys in the van sitting beside me that I didn't know. They looked as scared as I felt. Many were sobbing, shaking, asking each other, "What are we going to do? Where are they taking us? Are they going to kill us?"

Before the kidnappers dragged me into their crazy, civil war, my life was much different. I have many memories of peace in our home, and although everyone was poverty-stricken, there was respect and calm most of the time. We lived in a safe community where neighbours didn't live in fear, nor did they lock their doors. Our friends were more like family, and we often ate meals in each other's homes.

Life changed into something that is hard to imagine, a world where there was no peace or joy. Seeing the violence and death would affect my life for years to come and still does today at times. When I think back to the war, I don't know how I survived. Many of my friends were left lying in the fields, bodies strewn about like dead cattle.

My journey with pain and suffering began decades ago and thousands of kilometres away in Ethiopia. As a child soldier and then being addicted to alcohol was not part of anyone's dream for his or her life. Mine was a journey that unfolded into anguish and misery, unravelling further each day.

My family lived in a pleasant house, much nicer than others in our neighbourhood. We were poor and didn't have many material possessions, especially when compared to the luxuries in Canada, but we were happy. My dad, with the help of friends, built our home himself. Whenever it rained, the tin roof echoed the sound of the showers beating down upon it. Life was good back before the war began.

My friends and I went fishing in the early mornings nearly every day when there was no school. Mom would have the frying pan hot, waiting for me to get home to cook the fish for lunch. Swimming was a favourite past time, along with playing soccer with friends. We spent so much time outside in the blazing hot sun that our hair turned an orange-red colour.

Our dad worked hard as a manager at the port in Ethiopia, in charge of other men and shipping, an honest man who never drank alcohol or smoked. Even though he became angry at times, he had a soft, compassionate side that many people loved and respected. If we had room inside our home, dad would invite foreigners to stay with us whenever he saw them sleeping outside.

In our community, we all helped each other as best we could. Neighbours cut each other's hair, and we felt welcomed in each other's homes. We played together, ate together, and worked together. Nothing was yours growing up in our house. We shared clothes, shoes, and everything else we used when we played.

I don't remember the name of the game but we used to play outside with six holes lined up on the ground. Small rocks were our game-pieces, moving each rock from hole to hole until one person won by having them all. We didn't need expensive toys or other things to have fun with and laugh … we had each other.

Mom stayed and worked at home, taking care of my six brothers, two sisters, and me. She worked hard cooking, cleaning, washing clothes and everything else needed for a large family of ten. She loved us all equally and did her best to provide tender-love for our home and family.

I was about twelve when things suddenly changed for the worst when soldiers came into our neighbourhood and took young teenagers to fight in their civil war. It didn't matter how old the children were … they grabbed the tallest ones. My mom was always worried and frightened that one day they would kidnap one of her children. It was a terrifying thought that worried her every day.

Our family and neighbours talked a lot about the civil war. A friend of my brother shared stories with us about his time as a soldier, gun in hand. He told me about his nightmares and drinking alcohol to help him forget what he saw and felt. This war was cruel in so many ways …even making a mistake calling a General the wrong name resulted in being forced to dig a hole as high as one's head. And this was only one of the many punishments the teenage warriors experienced. When I was in bed at night, after hearing these stories, I thought about it a lot, and it scared me believing that one day I would be in these same nightmares of terror.

I was about eleven years old when the guerrillas came and abducted my oldest brother, Mohammed. Not hearing from him for six months, worried and distressed us all, especially my mom who succumbed to depression. She worried all the time about her son's well-being and safety. In despair, mom decided to search for him, we looked everywhere and found no trace of him, leaving us to fear the worst, that he has been injured, or worse, dead.

Dad became angry because we were spending all our money travelling around the countryside searching for my brother. Five years later my brother returned home, injured and a very different person. The war had taken a devastating toll on his mind and body. He had been shot in the leg by the enemy, and his mind had become confused and unhinged from drinking so much alcohol to numb the memories. It took a few months to heal his bullet-wounds, but he was a different person, not fit to return to fight.

Many of our neighbours suffered as we did, especially when their young sons never returned home or after being shot and injured. I heard so many war-stories that I didn't want to listen anymore … I already had enough nightmares about the risk of a soldier wounding or killing if they took me away.

Our Culture

My dad was an 'Imam' at our local mosque, the title of a worship leader. I was a Muslim and went to the mosque to learn the Quran. My teacher said something I didn't like one day,so I picked up a rock and threw it, hitting him in the head. The teacher told me not to come back again, but mom went and talked to him and I was allowed to return At only six or seven years old, I had memorized the Quran, something that was not easy to do for most of the young people in our community.

When I was ten, I remember my dad getting me to touch a woman who was sick, when I reached out and touched her with my hand, she got well. My dad said I had a divine gift from God and had me try to heal another woman. She was very sick, but when I touched her, she became well too. Many more people started showing up in the morning but I told my dad I was not comfortable doing it, so I stopped.

I wasn't aware of spirituality at such a young age, so I didn't know how the women were healed. I was only ten or eleven years old. When I look back now, I understand that it's God's power, which heals, not mine. So, even though I didn't know Jesus at the time I was touching the women, I do believe it was a legitimate healing. I often visited with Christian believers in their home, singing songs, and listening to them at Bible studies, talking about Jesus. They spoke about the birth of Jesus and I wanted to know more. Even though I was a Muslim, I learned about Jesus; and I believe His spirit was in my heart when touching the women.

We had many Christian neighbours, and when they celebrated their holidays, they invited us to join them for dinner. They respected our Muslim doctrine of not eating pork and served vegetables, but when we invited them over to our home, they ate what we served. Once in a while I would go to a friend's house and eat … not telling my family I was eating unholy food.

My aunt was the only Christian in our family, and she said that she often prayed for us. I heard about the Bible and the story of Jesus from Christian neighbours and my aunt, but we had the religion that we followed as a family, and if we were to leave it, we would lose our family. Alcohol and other intoxicants are forbidden in the Quran, as they are a bad habit that drives people away from the remembrance of God.

I drank some alcohol once and vomited. My mom covered up for me so my dad wouldn't know about my foolishness and rebellion. While I was in the bedroom, I could hear them talking, dad insisting that he see and speak to me. As dad walked toward the bedroom, my mom said:

"No, come with me, you don't need to go in the bedroom."

Dad replied, "No, no, I need to get something," Mom responded with, "No, come on, I need to tell you about something."

After she returned and cleaned up the mess that I had made, she said, "Jemal, you are so lucky your dad didn't find you." Dad left the house for a while, and then returned with his nose in the air. "What's that smell, has someone been drinking?" Nobody answered, and he stopped talking about it.

Peter and I still drank, but not at home. We would meet after school and chew 'Chat' before drinking. 'Chat' grew in areas around Ethiopia … a leafy plant that gave me a feeling of drinking strong coffee or chewing coca leaves. It was our culture in Ethiopia to use, and it made us feel, like a high.

Dad worked all day and insisted that everyone had to be home to sit down and eat dinner together. Even though our school was miles away, we had to be there, if you weren't there, you didn't eat.

Our home and culture were not much different from others in our community. When you took the clothes off that you were wearing, someone else that needed them could use them. Living in a poor country, with six brothers and two sisters, we wore what the cleanest clothes were.

A few thousand people lived in our village and had small family farms, raising chickens and other animals for food. We had about twenty sheep and thirty goats on our land. I took care of them for a few years as a young boy. When I was older, my younger brother took over. Even though we went about our daily lives doing chores, having fun, and enjoying family time, fears of the military actions were on our minds more often than not.

One year after they took my brother Mohammed, my other brother, Ali was next in line. However, he had a work permit to work on a ship, so they let him stay working. Mom and dad waited as long as they could before telling the military so that they wouldn't take anyone else from our family. My brother and I didn't want to go, and dad agreed, so we planned that we would leave the family to escape on a ship that was leaving the harbour soon. Sounded like a good idea at the time, just run away and hide from my fears of having to fight in the war, but it was not to be. My life would soon turn into a hellish-nightmare that I wouldn't wish on anyone.

With dad's permission, I attempted my first stow-away on a ship out of Ethiopia. My friend and I went down to the shipyard, days, weeks, and months on end to find out when the next ship was leaving port. Finally, we found a ship that was leaving Africa.

I didn't tell my mom I was going to attempt another stow away that night because I knew she would try to stop me. It broke my heart to leave her but I felt like this was the only way to avoid being captured and forced into the military.

It took us about four hours to swim out to the ship and climb up the anchor chain, but the locked hatch prevented us from climbing up, so we swam back to shore. Looking back over the water, we saw another group of swimmers on their way to the same ship and told them it was impossible. We informed them that we could not climb aboard because of the closed anchor door, but they wouldn't believe us. Back on land, we heard the ship's engine start, preparing to leave. A few days later, we saw five dead, decomposing bodies. I had failed in my futile attempt to escape, but I would try again.

As a young teenager trying to find my way in life, my days often felt like I was living in an awkward vacuum. Some moments my mind filled with distress, jumping from this to that, sometimes exploding into chaos and fear.

Chapter 2

Failed Escape and Death

Terrified Tears

The Ethiopian civil war conflict was brutal and barbaric. Countless teenagers became slaves and dragged into guerrilla factions. At times, it was brother fighting against brother. There was no sleep, for weeks at a time. I began to know what hunger was, stumbling along for countless miles with no food. When they did feed us, we ate crackers, bread, and sardines, just enough to keep us alive and hold a gun. I kept thinking, "How are we going to get out of here alive?" The gunfire and fighting went on and on what seemed like forever.

"If you don't shoot your gun at the enemy, we will kill you," yelled an angry soldier.

I kept thinking, "Why am I here ... who am I fighting, what am I fighting for?"

The sounds of firing bullets and explosions deafened my ears. It was gruesome seeing so much war and bloodshed. Innocent people lying dead on the roads and in the bushes, body parts torn away. These massacres implanted horrific memories in my mind. The horrors of war and chaos created suffering everywhere, tearing families apart.

Trucks took us to a warehouse and then transferred us to different places, wherever they needed us to fight. Military training was near non-existent, just point, try to aim and shoot. We were filthy, never changing our socks or shaving, bearing scruffy-looking, dirty beards. Sleep escaped me, and when I did want to close my eyes, I would ask a friend to keep an eye out for me because we were on the front lines in the war. If the enemy had a chance, they would shoot us. Even the officers in our army would kill us if we disobeyed them.

We walked for miles up into the mountains and down in the desert, so hard and stressful beyond words. I worked with and helped many young child-soldiers, some older and some younger than me. We would encourage one another, telling each other that it was going to be okay. We talked about being back home, and the fun stuff that would distract our minds from where we were and what we were doing. Somehow, we were going to get through this. The new soldiers arrived shaking and crying. I put a towel on the head of one child, holding his hand, and said, "Don't worry, we'll get through this." Another one was screaming and choking from shock. I tried to calm them as best I could, telling them whatever I felt they needed to hear.

I didn't want to shoot or kill anyone … these bullets brought death to my friends, the people I played with as kids, and their neighbours. We were all citizens of the same country, but that didn't matter, we fought against each other for the control of political power. It was a civil revolution with no end in sight.

One young person I knew who was with us, had a brother on the other side that we were fighting. When we took over their area, we found him dead, lying on the ground. His mind told him that he had killed his brother and went crazy, very crazy. He threw his gun and took off his jacket. The soldiers took him away, and we never saw him again. While standing there in front of this madness, I told my friend, "We must get out of this nightmare, or we'll go crazy as he did." When I close my eyes today and think back to this day, I can still feel, taste, and see this scene playing in my mind like a movie as I hold back terrified tears.

I don't know how many enemies, child-soldiers I shot and killed … it's an awful thing to think about and almost impossible to describe or imagine. Once I took my first life, it seemed to get easier …the fear was gone, someone was standing one minute, and then suffocating to death in blood the next.

I had no contact with my family for over a year. As with many, they thought I was dead because countless child soldiers never return home.

After marching through many little villages, they allowed us to rest, have lunch, and walk around for a couple of hours. The town had a few roads, and the soldiers couldn't see where we were most of the time. Peter and I decided this was the time to escape. When we were sure nobody was watching us, off we went, running down the road to freedom.

My Next Escape, Prison and Death

We walked a long way before seeing a camel rider and another person walking to Djibouti on business. We asked if we could go with them, they accepted our guns as payment because we had no money. We threw away our military clothes and changed our clothes into some of theirs, which helped us blend in with them on the journey. They gave us food, water and we made it to Djibouti alive, but we didn't have any identification papers or passports. We often had to run from the police while staying in the port area until one person came to our rescue, allowing us to sleep in his boat. We helped paint and do other work for him, and remained there for a couple of months, waiting for a ship that was leaving port.

Finally, after waiting what seemed like forever, we climbed onto a large cargo ship, loaded with containers. When we found out the ship was going back to Ethiopia, we stayed in Djibouti. What a mistake that was! The authorities captured us and dragged us off to prison for four months.

In prison, food was scarce, meaning we had to fight for the meagre scraps that the guards placed on the filthy floor, everyone scrambling for each tiny morsel, just trying to survive. At first, we didn't know there wasn't much food, so we went hungry. Over the next few days, we were prepared to fight for survival. There was too little food for too many men, and I fought hard for each meal … it was fight or starve. The other prisoners began to complain that we were beating them up when the food arrived, so the guards moved us to another part of the prison.

When our time in jail was up, they planned to deport us, but there was a mix up in the paperwork. When we left the prison, we tried staying in the downtown area and hid from police. We still had no papers, and if they caught us, they would send us on a ship back home. We begged for food every day from the local people and slept near the port at night.

We needed new shoes but had no money to buy them, but we found a way. When people attended the mosque on Friday, everyone would take off their shoes. We would look for our sizes and put a new pair on our feet. After the mosque meeting, worshippers would go back to their community and homes. They were generous and gave us some leftover food they had from their weekly celebration. Each day was a matter of survival, and we did whatever we had to do just to stay alive.

After about a week out of prison, we met a person at the port who offered us work and provided a place for us to stay in one of the boats. Our job was transporting tourists, washing, painting, and doing maintenance work as needed.

Most of the local people we met in Djibouti hated Ethiopians. They told us to leave their country and go back home. They talked and dressed very different from us so they could instantly see we were from somewhere else. Although we were Muslims as they were, it didn't matter … they treated us with anger and disgust. They regarded tourists much differently, better than us, saying nothing negative against them. I never understood why, wishing they would change their words and actions towards us and treat us as they treated others … as equals.

We stayed a while longer in Djibouti before trying to return to our war-torn home in Ethiopia. Whenever the police would come by we would jump in the water and swim away from shore. They would yell at us, but not come out into the water. It was horrible and sad to see so many people die trying to stow-away. Of course, we were scared, but we still attempted to escape because it was better than being in the military, killing your friends and neighbours.

Finally, we had our chance to stow-away on another ship. Other people joined us, and we all swam for about an

hour. We waited until dark to climb up the ship's anchor chain and then hid until it left port. As soon as the ship started moving out to sea, we came out from hiding to find some food. It was not long before they caught us and put us to work. Surprisingly, they were kind to us and treated us well. The ship arrived in Israel where we tried to go ashore, but they refused us entry into their country. Even though we claimed to be Ethiopian Jews, we faced severe scrutiny. We couldn't speak Hebrew, so they gave us a translator, asking us many questions, trying to find out the truth.

"Where are you from," they asked.

"We are Ethiopian Jews," I replied.

"Ok, what tribe are you from?" We didn't answer.

"You're not Jews," they insisted.

I knew that we were in trouble and said, "Oh well, we tried."

After immigration said they wouldn't accept us as refugees, the ship's captain was angry, as we were. The next destination was Japan, but they wouldn't welcome us there either because Japan didn't accept refugees.

One night, a few days out from the port of Israel, the captain woke us up in the middle of the night and said we had to get off the ship. It was cold and dark. We had thoughts of rage, thinking about fighting the crew. There were five of us, my friend and I from the military, and three other boys who had stowed away on the ship.

We told the captain, "No, we're not jumping off the ship!"

He replied, "Either you get off my ship, or we'll shoot you where you stand and throw your dead bodies off the ship!" Two of my friends said, "No, we're not going to get off the ship." The captain picked up his gun and said, "You have to get off the ship, or you're going to die." All the ship's crew was standing there to help the captain if he needed it. We had no other choice.

The captain stopped the ship's propellers so it would not suck us up into certain death. The giant hull slowly came to a halt, and we jumped, swimming away. As the ship disappeared into the night, five of us began screaming at each other in the dark.

When morning arrived over the horizon, we couldn't see land. The sun was blazing hot, reflecting off the salty water. We had no idea where to swim. Some people were sobbing, tears rolling down their face, others crying aloud as they splashed about in the sea. I tried to help two people who were tired, telling them to hold onto my shoulder. I carried them in tow for as long as possible, but the situation was worsening, and I had to think about myself … conserve my energy by whatever means possible.

The hot sun reflected off the salt water, my friend's flesh stuck to my shoulders, peeling off in pieces as I swam. Eventually, I told them I was too exhausted … too empty of energy to carry on. They slid their hand off my shoulder, and I watched them sink down into the water, disappearing into the depths of darkness. Three out of the five of us drowned over the next two days. The feelings inside my mind tore away at my heart … such painful memories would haunt me for decades.

The wind kept pushing us, and eventually, we landed on Jamal al-Tair Island beach where there was a signal lighthouse. Exhausted and hungry, we collapsed down and fell asleep on the shore. When I woke up, I walked a little way and found a dugout area with water. I tried a sip to taste if there was salt in it. It was good, so I drank, washed my face and woke Peter.

The next day, with no shoes on, we climbed up to the lighthouse that was on top of the sheer rock. It was painful and hard, but we did find a bit of food. After a few more days stranded somewhere unknown to us, we found a fisherman who came to shore in a boat, searching for water. I didn't speak his language, but my friend did, so we told him we wanted to go back to Ethiopia and he agreed to take us. The boat's engine was broken, so we sailed. Mercy was on our side it seemed.

A German freighter almost ran us over, but stopped and allowed us to climb aboard. We told our whole story, and the captain agreed to take us all, and the fishing boat. The ship was on course for Germany and for some reason the company that owned the boat said, "No, these refugees cannot go."

The captain gave us food and water, then lowered our boat into the water and left. A few days later, another large fishing boat came upon us and agreed to help, attaching a rope to our boat so they could tow it behind theirs.

We still didn't have any identity documents, so they thought we were on the same side of the military action. Although the captain told them we came from the island he found us on, they didn't believe us and put us in their Massawa prison for six months.

It was not like any prison I had never seen, heard about or been in before It was horrible! The prison wardens unceremoniously buried those who died there, and the government rarely notified the next of kin. Children, and those over the military service-age of forty, they detained for what seemed like forever just because they could.

The food was ghastly, smelled and looked like washing-up water. It consisted of bread, lentils, and half-cooked unsalted cabbage in tiny portions. They served it in a communal bowl in our cell where we had to eat with our hands. We had tap water to drink, but not enough. There was an open toilet in the cell. We could only wash once every two weeks and slept on the damp floor with only two thin blankets. Many prisoners held in crowded underground cells, rarely saw daylight, many suffered from diarrhea and other sicknesses.

Torture is not something I like to remember or talk about today. How could anyone forget such a thing? How could I ever forgive such evil against another human being? For six long months, they pulled us out of our cells and took us to the torture room. The guards thought we were spies, so they came into our prison cells at night and took us away one at a time.

They sat me on a chair, tied my hands behind my back, and then pushed the chair backwards onto the floor so my feet would be facing them, up in the air. The guard peeled the skin off the poisonous tail of a large stingray fish, the size of a rope, and used it to whip the bottom of my feet. I screamed as they beat my feet, my head and body. The severe pain lasted for hours, making it hard to walk back to my cell once they were done.

We only had naps during the day because we lay awake at night knowing they would drag us away again at any minute. I would plead with them, "We are not spies, and we're from the same country as you … why do you hate us so much?" However, it didn't matter.

The Eritrea military wanted to take over the prison, so they attacked and destroyed it. It was total chaos with the prison walls exploding from missiles and bombs, prisoners and guards running around screaming. As we ran away from the destruction, I looked back, saw the crumbled walls, and smoke in the air. It was scary and traumatizing to see and feel such destruction and violence happening all around us. Nobody knew where we were running to; I just followed people in front of me until finally arriving at the port where they allowed a few of us to board a ship heading back to Ethiopia. There were far too many people trying to escape with us, and there wasn't enough room for all. The ship couldn't take everyone … the others were left behind to fend for themselves.

Chapter 3

Back Home in Ethiopia

It was three years since I was first kidnapped from school and forced to fight in the military … I was now nineteen years old. When we arrived at the Ethiopian port where my dad worked, he was surprised to see me, questioning whether it truly was me. There was crying, and even more tears when I arrived home to see my family and friends. They thought I was dead. They were so sure that I was not coming back alive, they'd had a funeral for me with mourners.

As I walked home, my mom saw me and dropped to the ground, crying. She was so emotional when she saw me, not really believing I was alive. The neighbours gathered around her, trying to console and help. Mom lost it, is how I remember her state of emotions. I guess it was so hard for her because she had already cried a lot when thinking I was dead, and now she was crying tears of happiness when I returned home alive.

For three days mom went to her bedroom because she was crying so much. She lay on the bed, suffering from headaches, confusion … and happiness all at the same time. I know it was hard for mom to think I was dead, and then accept that I was alive. I knew she was happy, but seeing her cry so much, made me feel sad and emotional.

While I was gone, my mom was so sad, scared and depressed because she always thought the military was going to come back and take another one of her children away as they did to me.

My home was not the same as before. I felt like I didn't belong there anymore. My mind didn't let me sleep at night, and I questioned God about my life … every thought went in a circle and back to the beginning over and over again, with no end.

My dad encouraged me to start going to the Mosque to help clear my mind and order my thoughts, but it just kept getting worse. I hung around the bar all the time and drank. I missed my friends … they had all died horrible deaths and I remembered every one. I wondered why I had to go through all that horror at such a young age. So many of my friends had tried to escape and ended up dying a horrible death. Many people came to my home and asked me how I did it all … how did I survive? The young kids, ten or eleven years old, wanted to learn how to stowaway on a ship to avoid the same nightmares as I experienced in the war.

Every day, questions and more questions reminded me of the horrors I endured. I thought about my childhood friends that had been taken to other war zones or were left lying in military hospital beds, suffering from horrific injuries.

After I returned home from the war, my dad decided to retire from work, open a family restaurant and store. It was about a two-hour drive from where we lived in our village. I wasn't doing anything at the time and dad asked me to work with him.

The business, attached to a home, is where we ate and slept. People in this community spoke a different language, but my dad could understand, and I could communicate enough with the customers. I didn't feel like going there to work, but my mom encouraged and convinced me, "Go with your dad, it will be good for you." At first, it was ok, but not for long.

For six months, I enjoyed working with my dad until the night I came home from the bar, seeing my dad and a woman in bed together. "Oh no," I thought … anger was raging in my mind. When my dad saw me looking into the bedroom, he was shocked! Later that evening, he was nervous around me and avoided talking to me, and the next morning when he tried speaking to me, I said, "No, I'm not in the mood," and walked away, disgusted, angry and confused.

The women tried talking to me, saying, "We are in love, blah, blah, blah," and I replied, "Don't you know my dad is married, what are you doing?"

In the Muslim faith, you can have three or more wives, but your first wife must first agree to it. The marriages have to be official, telling all your family members and children. What my dad and this woman were doing was not okay.

I used to look up to my dad as a community leader and spiritual man in our Mosque, but after seeing what he did, I was so angry and resentful, I stopped believing and didn't go to the Mosque anymore.

I told my dad, "I am done working with you," and returned home to live at our family home. He tried to stop me, but I stood firm in my decision. A few hours later, my dad showed up at our family home.

I was sitting down when he walked in, and I had not told my mom about the affair, but I could tell by the look on my dad's face that he thought I had. Even when my mom asked why I returned home, I didn't tell her the real reason, "I do not want to work there anymore, mom … that's it."

Dad took my mom into a back room bedroom where I could hear them talking, him blaming me for not working hard enough. Later that night I could hear them yelling and fighting … dad began getting physical with mom. As soon as I saw this, I got in between them and pushed dad back and said, "No way, do not touch my mom or behave that way towards her!" We never did talk about it again, and dad returned to the business the next day.

Shortly after I experienced all this, I stowed away on another ship, leaving my community behind.

Our local government didn't know we were back yet and I knew that we had to disappear before they discovered our return and forced us to fight again. A short while later I found out that there was a Greek ship leaving port soon. I told Peter that we had to go right away. However, that night we were fighting in a bar and the police arrested Peter and threw him in jail. We were different people than we were before. We didn't go to school … our life consisted of drinking and fighting much of the time. I tried to get my friend out of jail but I couldn't. Since it seemed we were destined to go our separate ways, I stowed away on another ship, leaving him behind.

The Ethiopia port was locked-up tight, and the ship that I wanted to climb aboard was leaving soon. As I climbed across a rope tied to the ship from the dock, I looked back and saw another person, someone I knew, following me. John and I climbed over the railing, went into the engine room, and stood in dirty oil up to our necks. In fear of being found by the crew, we stayed there until we started moving.

The next day we heard a loud horn blast and knew we were heading out to sea. As soon as we felt the ship moving, we crawled out from hiding, covered in slimy oil. We found a shower to clean up in and went searching for some food, but they caught us. It seemed like my life was always on a journey of escape, avoiding capture, and eventually captured again.

One angry crewmember slapped me in the face. We were already eight hours away from the port, and the captain didn't want to turn around to drop us off, so he told his crew to find us a place to stay on the ship.

The captain gave us work, handed us food, and we had a dry, warm place to sleep. When we stopped in Egypt, he hid us, not telling anyone that he had stowaways, telling us to stay quiet in our room. After leaving Egypt, my friend, who could speak some English, talked with the captain a bit. We didn't know where we were going, and neither did the captain. We cruised near Greece and Italy, stopping only for fuel and supplies.

Finally, the company informed him about which country to head to and he told us the good news. We were on our way to Quebec, Canada! It was a long, three-month journey. The captain liked us, gave us cigarettes, one beer a day, and the crew treated us well. We scraped off old, rusty paint before painting a new coat, and did whatever else they wanted us to do. We were so happy and worked hard for him the next few months until we arrived in Quebec City, December 1989.

We didn't know much about Canada or Quebec before we arrived. Only through letters from those who had already been there before us did we learn a little bit. We heard it was a great, peaceful place, free from violence and war.

Today, when I think about my life as a child soldier, seeing death, torture in prison, and watching bodies floating dead in the sea, I still feel some of the pain I went through. How could I forget … how could anyone not remember such a traumatizing, emotional place? I wondered how I would ever be able to live with myself … function in this new world I was entering into, Canada. Was it possible, could I do it … would I be able to deal with my feeling of hate towards the guards who tortured me every week for six months? How could I ever forgive such evil? How could I forgive myself for killing young child soldiers?

Chapter 4

Life in Quebec

As we neared the shores of Canada, I was so scared, afraid of being deported back to a place that I once called home. Because of the language barrier, I was confused and didn't understand what they said … their French language was strange. It was frustrating and made me angry when people would ask me, "What did you say, what did you say, do you speak English or what?"

In Quebec City, they put us in a room, and when they took us to the bathroom, I looked for a way to escape, but there wasn't any.

Then Canada immigration placed us in a small prison-like cell until all the paperwork was ready. It was stressful, but we did have a warm place to sleep. The captain of the ship we arrived on bought us new clothes for the cold weather in Canada and even gave us pocket money. I was so happy and warm having a big winter coat. Winter in Quebec is long and extremely cold from November through March, similar to what I imagined Moscow or Siberia to be. Deep snow piled up everywhere, like a massive, white blanket covering the roads and sidewalks.

After waiting in Quebec City for a while, immigration told us they were taking us on a plane. We were paranoid, scared, and did not believe or trust them. Why would I, my trust and faith in people was gone? We were ready to run, thinking they would send us to the Ethiopian embassy for deportation. It was so exhausting being scared all the time and not knowing what was going to happen next.

After they processed us in Montreal, we met a man that spoke our language. He told us that everything was going to be okay and not to worry. Canada immigration took our pictures and then I began to understand what was happening. I could finally relax and sleep, knowing I was going to remain safe and free in Canada. What a relief.

Following one and a half months at the YMCA, we received checks to find a place to rent in Montreal. The biggest challenge for me living in Canada was the loneliness. At the YMCA hotel, there were many people to have dinner and socialize with, but when I moved to my own place, it was just my T.V. and me.

I called home and told my family what had happened. I wanted to talk to my mom, but my family kept saying she was outside somewhere or at the market. After a few months, it became clear to me that my family didn't want to or were afraid to tell me what had happened. I knew she was depressed … crying all the time because of losing my older brother and I was no longer around.

After many months of asking to speak with my mom, as is our culture and custom, they talked to my friend. The next day, in the morning, he told me that my mom had passed away. They informed me it was because I had left and she couldn't take it anymore. My mind agonized with guilt, and I felt responsible and ashamed. I was a mess for days after learning about my mom's passing. I began drinking in the bar, trying to shut down my mind.

The heat in my tiny Montreal home was not working when I first moved in, so I froze more often than not. I remember going to get some groceries and falling on the ice on the way back home. I just laid there for a minute until an old woman poked me with her cane. I don't know what she said, but I think she wanted me to get up and go. My eggs broke, and everything was all over in the snow and ice. I will never forget that first winter. I tried to adjust as best I could to the cold, and had thoughts of going to immigration and asking them to send me to a warmer place. Compared to living in hot Africa, Quebec was the complete opposite, a deep freeze that burned your face, ears and lips.

Once I settled in Canada, I began to have a new dream, not of being a soccer player or movie star but learning English and French. I saw myself as still being young enough and able to succeed in school. I wanted an education, but after only two days in classes, deep fear overwhelmed me. My mind went back to living in Ethiopia, in the military when I was a child.

There were so many books and so much pressure that I told them I couldn't return to class because of something in my past. Even before I started classes, I couldn't sleep because I knew I was going to school the next day. My memories haunted me so much, so I didn't learn English or French in a Canadian school. I learned from the streets and bars by listening to people talking. Nobody coached me on English. I would sit there at the bar and try to speak English, or at my job by listening to others.

In the summer, I moved downtown and tried again to take French classes to learn French so that I could receive an extra hundred dollars more each month, but it was impossible for me to learn. After attending classes for only three days, I couldn't continue. My mind often lived in visions of violence, torture, shootings, and death all around me.

My neighbour from Saudi Arabia had a car wash and asked me if I wanted a job. I said yes, started working for one dollar a car, and received tips from happy customers. It was the summer of 1990, my new beginning in Canada. I met many people at the carwash, and my boss allowed me to drink alcohol while doing my job. I didn't make much money during that winter, but I continued working there until the following summer. "What else am I going to do in this foreign land," I thought.

When I had money, I would drink at home … then go to the bar to get away from being alone. The loneliness hit me for a few months until I started looking for another job following the cold winter. Working at the carwash was okay for a while, but I began to have feelings and thoughts about killing myself. Although I liked living in Canada with no fear of civil war and violence, I just wanted to shut down everything … die to my pain and thoughts. What a mess my life was at such a young age.

Back home in Ethiopia, there was always family and everyone sleeping near each other, you were never alone. I was having such a hard time in Canada that I called home often, missing them a lot. I lost it the first few months to the point of insanity … but I didn't dare or have the courage to take my own life. I couldn't do it.

I lived in Montreal for three years before receiving my Canadian passport. Back then, it was easy to become a Canadian. There were just a few classes you had to take which were simple.

I met a person from Eritrea who owned a restaurant, and he asked me to work as a dishwasher for him. After six months of washing pots, pans, and dishes, he started to teach me to cook. When the cook quit, I got the job.

The seafood restaurant was big and could sit over three hundred people where over the next few years I learned how to cook everything. I did everything a cook did and didn't even have to go to school to learn how to do it.

Later, when the person who trained me left, I took over his job as the head cook. It was great. I was so happy at my job … but not all was good for very long as my personal life deteriorated.

The Curse of Alcohol

I began drinking more and more … and was usually quite drunk by the end of my workday. A friend, who also cooked there, would go out to the local bar with me to drink even more. Why not, it was a cheap way to forget my past and have fun.

I had a close Muslim friend whose house I would go to on Fridays. We would go to the Mosque in the evening, and then go out to drink. I didn't read the Quran anymore and only did my prayers on Friday. I did participate in Ramadan and stayed away from alcohol for one month, but it was hard.

I went to the bar when I was lonely, which was more often than not, finding other lonely people just like me. When I drank or was drunk, it was easier to meet people, but I lived a confusing, sad life with sleepless nights and horrible dreams.

Whenever I closed my eyes, I could see everything that happened in the war … as if I was right there again, hearing the gunfire kept me awake. My nightmares were much worse now than when I was in the military. Alcohol helped me drift off at times or pass out. A few drinks only detached my mind and gave fragmented relief, so I drank more. Little did I know at the time that my psychological trauma combined with alcohol would lead to enormous trouble?

Nobody understood what was going on in my mind, nor did I share much with people ... I didn't want to talk about it. My life became worse and worse. I was in an escape mode ... my brain just couldn't process what happened in my past. My thinking was hijacked and frozen.

As hard as it was, I tried to focus on survival and self-protection. I felt helpless, my emotions ran wild, experiencing fatigue, anxiety, and I was startled by loud noises ... like my heart stopped dead for a moment. Sometimes my senses were on hyper-alert, dominating my life, robbing me of joy and pleasure.

One evening while I was at a party in Montreal, I met a girl, and we talked. We exchanged phone numbers, and she came to the restaurant where I worked. We often met after my shift at the mall nearby, and we started dating.

She was Ethiopian Jewish and didn't tell her parents that I was Muslim. She said that my last name was Brahan, and I was a Christian. If they knew I was Muslim, our relationship was not going to work. I didn't stop her from telling them I was a Christian, and I was okay with it. When I revealed this to my brothers and sisters in Ethiopia, they stopped talking to me because of her being Jewish.

Her brother, sister, and mother lived in Israel, and one day they unexpectedly asked me if I was Muslim. When

I said yes, it was crazy, and I didn't know what to think or do about it.

Then we found out my girlfriend was pregnant. After being pregnant for six months, we decided to get married. When I called home to ask my father for his blessing, I told him she was from Ethiopia, and he asked me what her religion was. When I told him she was Jewish, he lost it and hung up on me. I called back, and he wouldn't talk to me. He wanted me to get married to a Muslim.

I don't know why, but I was surprised at how angry he was and how he didn't respect or accept my choices. He wasn't innocent after having an affair while married to my mom, "Why should he care," I thought. Today, if I were in the same situation I would comfort myself with Exodus 14:14 the Lord will fight for you, you shall hold your peace.

One of my brothers moved to Germany and married a Christian lady, and I didn't judge him as my father did to me. Even my brother and sister in Ethiopia still would not talk to me. I used to send my family money occasionally, even though they shunned me.

Sometimes doing the right thing may not seem fair but I know that God sees the good we do. Colossians 3: 17, 23 "And whatever you do in word or deed, do all in the name of the Lord Jesus, giving thanks to God the Father through Him. And whatever you do, do it heartily, as to the Lord and not to men..."

After our baby was born, I stopped drinking for a while but not for long. People would give us alcohol as gifts when they came to see the baby, and I started drinking again.

I have warm memories of celebrating our daughter's first birthday at our restaurant. I taught her how to walk and speak her first word in Amharic. She would sit and watch me cook and ask if she could help. It was fun spending so much time with her, playing and eating deserts together. I loved her so much, but I think I could have been a better father if only I knew how..

My wife worked at an Ethiopian restaurant as a cook, and I would pick our daughter up from daycare, but was always late. I was finished work at 3 pm and immediately started drinking, and would not arrive to pick up our child until 5-6 pm. One day I was so late, the daycare told me it was the last time they would put up with it from me.

In 1994, almost one year after our daughter was born we both quit our jobs. We got a loan, borrowed some money from her family, and used our savings to open our Ethiopian restaurant. We both cooked and I waited on tables.

Our restaurant had a license to serve alcohol, and I wouldn't go home after work … drinking, of course. I even slept the night there sometimes. We were open six days a week, and on Monday, we closed, but we would buy supplies and food, so really, we worked seven days a week.

For the first few years, we struggled financially with the business. I was still drinking much of the time, and we fought often. I was with other women, cheating on my wife. She gave me many chances and opportunities to stop drinking and change. She worked the day shift, and I would do the evening. Finally, she gave me one final opportunity to choose between her and my daughter or the alcohol. I chose alcohol.

The memory of my father cheating on my mom haunted me for many years no matter where I ran away too. When I look back at what my dad did, I wonder if my womanizing and drinking was a result of what happened … the pain and trauma of witnessing it.

I don't remember my dad being an emotional man, nor did he give me much attention, love or sit down with me and talk about things in life that would help me along. I loved my dad, but I didn't learn much from him about how to be a good husband or father to my children. Maybe this is part of the reason I eventually abandoned my wife and daughter. I know my addiction to alcohol is the main reason, but perhaps my drinking related, in part, to not having a dad to teach me.

I never knew how to be a father to my daughter. Our marriage and relationship were full of the garbage I had brought with me from Ethiopia. Being so sick inside my mind, I couldn't see anything good around me. I didn't know how to behave, react, be a friend to my wife, or even how to love somebody. Being so lonely, confused and frustrated pushed me into drinking more. How could I be normal when I didn't know what normal was?

I worked hard, but without alcohol, I couldn't sleep or seemingly function. After closing time at the restaurant, I would still be drinking. When we opened in the morning, I started drinking again. Sometimes I drank too much and blacked out, not remembering what I had done. That is when the problems began to kill my family life and marriage. I started forgetting things, and my mind was blank. It was if things didn't happen. Everybody was talking about my drinking behind my back.

I just wanted out ... to run away and start over again. Bad dreams and horrific nightmares about my past always happened when I was not drinking. When I drank, I could sleep and not have the visions. When I passed out, my mind was asleep, on pause.

Leaving my Wife and Child

Finally, I jumped on a bus to Toronto, but after one week away, a person called my wife and told her where I was. She came on the bus and brought me back home. She said to me, "We can do this," and we did for a while, but it didn't last. How could it, I was still doing the same thing as before I left ... nothing changed. That trip was the extent of my travelling in Canada, just before I left for Oregon.

While living in Montreal, I would visit my friend Joe, who I was in prison with at Djibouti. He went to school in Canada and learned how to fix computers. He had a wife

51

and kids, and they let me stay a couple of days with them. It was not long before I wanted to leave again. This time was different though. I talked to Peter, who lived in Portland Oregon and decided to take my passport and travel all the way there by train.

I had made the decision to leave because I thought I was going to hurt my wife and daughter if I continued to be with them while I was drinking so much. When I am drunk, I am a different person than who I am today.

I wrote my wife a note and left my key on the counter. It was painful leaving my wife and daughter behind. I wanted to deal with my past, but the terrible memories of what happened to me in Ethiopia were just too painful. My wife knew most of my history, but we never talked about it or tried to work through it. I kept myself away from everyone who wanted to get close to me. She offered to send me to counselling to deal with my past, but I never wanted to go. My ingrained culture was that you deal with things on your own, fix it yourself, do not show weakness.

Another reason I left was to avoid getting into trouble with the law or being arrested for fighting. When I drank too much, heartache followed me. I would fight people and be injured, needing stitches to close the wounds. It didn't seem right or wise to stay with my wife and daughter. Perhaps I was making excuses to justify leaving.

I was on the train for three days and four nights, asking myself if I had done the right thing by leaving. They served alcohol, my pain reliever, so I was drunk much of the trip. I missed my daughter already, and it hurt not being able to see or talk to her. The only thing I had of her was in my wallet … a picture of her at three months old, and I still have it today. I thought about my life in Canada. I thought about my wife and daughter home alone without me. I was struggling with thoughts to the point of anger and depression.

My mind kept going back and forth, like two voices talking to me. I drank to forget all that stuff and, partying on the train with people I met kept me sane. My thoughts about going to Oregon were just to take a break, I had no intentions of staying in the US for long. I wanted to visit my friend and then come back to Canada.

Chapter 5

My Oregon Nightmare

I arrived in Oregon to find Peter and all his friends drinking at raging parties ... a scene that I was all too familiar with back in Montreal. We spent many hours catching up, and my friend soon saw that I had a severe drinking problem. He told me that I drank excessively because, before breakfast, I already had a beer in my hand. It was a rough neighbourhood, not like where I lived before in Canada.

One evening I called a pizza place, and they refused my order, saying they would not deliver after 8 pm because it was too dangerous. It seemed odd to me at the time, but I would soon learn why some hesitated to walk around here in the dark shadows.

There was no problem fitting in with other people like me who drank every night. I began to run his house for him, bringing all kinds of shady people over. "Slow down, take it easy, my friend," he pleaded as I staggered around the house.

Waking up in the mornings, I'd feel sick, hung over until more alcohol calmed down my shaking body and running mind. Rather than think about my past, I thought about where I would like to live and what I wanted to do. It was a lot warmer here in the winter months, so I decided to stay and live in America, but my friends told me I would probably have to marry someone to live here.

I met a woman about ten years older than me, and we began dating. She worked hard and provided me with alcohol, cigarettes, and other things I wanted or needed. Finally, I asked her if she wanted to get married and she asked me if I was serious. She didn`t know I just wanted to marry her so I could stay living in America and said, "Ok, yes I'll marry you." We were both drunk the next day when we listened to, "For better or for worse…" and we affirmed, "I do." I was hoping 'for the better,' but it was not to be for very long. Soon after, my wife sold one of her homes, began spending all the money, and I got a job.

I was earning enough money to buy what I needed, and it was okay working there until my boss told me, "Jemal, you're drinking too much, and it's not safe for you to keep working for me." After losing my job, my wife asked me to slow down my drinking, but it wasn't possible for me to do. All of my life I seemed to go sideways, up, down, and crazy. I got to the point where I didn't care anymore about my life or the people around me … each new day was the same as yesterday with a drink in my hand. My wife begged me to go to a treatment centre, and when she talked to me about it, I'd leave, visit my friend, watch TV and get drunk.

My ex-wife in Canada would call and leave messages for me, pleading for me to come back and take care of my daughter. It was the last thing on my mind. I didn't want to think about my daughter or talk to anyone about my life in Montreal.

"If you quit drinking for one entire day, I'll buy you anything you want to eat … pizza or whatever," my friend promised. Of course, I refused the challenge, not caring about food or anything else offered as a reward to do something other than drinking. Talking to someone about my problems was too painful to think about. I tried not to re-live the trauma. My life was spiralling down into darkness, and it would get worse, much worse. I started hanging around people who were doing cocaine.

We would put it in our pockets, go to the bathroom and get high, come back out to our partying friends, and drink some more. This toxic combination gave me a buzz and a headache at the same time. My wife didn't see or hear from me for days … my brain was too messed up to go home.

One day my wife said that I needed to go and finish my immigration paperwork soon. It was my third time making this appointment, and I was so shaky that I needed to keep drinking just to function. She said, "No, immigration will smell the alcohol, and you might not get your green card." I said okay, but the day before we went to the immigration office, there was a party, and she found me with another girl. I tried to hide her so my wife wouldn't know, but she came in and saw her in the bedroom, ran out the door and left. My hopes of immigration and a green card were now dead.

When I arrived home the next day, my wife asked me what I wanted to do. She said I could rent the house and she would move to Texas. My new girlfriend moved in with me, and my wife walked out, simple as that. Our home quickly became a party house and a place for gang members and drugs. People were in and out all day and night. I looked at myself as being a 'functioning addict' until I started using crack cocaine ... a drug that was like riding a lightning bolt, then crashing to earth not long after each hit.

When my friend drove by and saw what was happening, I said that I was living the dream. He said, "What are you doing, do you want to go to jail in America?" He always came and tried to look after me, but I didn't listen. I stopped dating the woman who moved in with me and started hanging out with others who had gang member friends. After we got to know each, I asked if I could join. They warned me that there would be questions and tests to see if they could trust me. Soon after, they accepted me into the fellowship of thugs and drug dealers. I was now in a gang and part of their family.

One day I woke up and began asking myself how I arrived in this terrible mess. There was too much drinking, weed smoking, hard drugs, and carrying guns. I was not 'living a new dream' … more like a nightmare. I loved pockets full of money, the parties, shiny cars, and being part of their gang family but it was scary. The hierarchy didn't dictate that the tallest and strongest was the leader or his close underlings. It was the meanest and most violent.

We used the house I was renting from my wife for everything, including cooking crack in the basement. The neighbours hated us with the constant cars, foot traffic, and loud noise around the clock.

Gangs and Guns

Peter came by and talked to me about what not to do and telling me how much I had changed for the worse. His girlfriend had heard dreadful things about me and told him what was going on. She was from the African American community I lived in and knew everything that was happening in this dangerous place with gangs on every block.

One summer day, two of our gang members went to another gangs turf and busted into their house. They pushed everyone on the floor and took all their money. Swift revenge happened the next day when two Cadillacs showed up in front of our house and started shooting at us.

They shot two of us, including me. We grabbed our guns and chased after them, and then returned home to hide all our stuff because we knew the police were on their way.

When the police arrived, they interrogated us, wrote notes about us telling them, "We don't know why this happened ...we were sitting here, not doing anything to provoke a gun fight." Of course, I didn't tell the police all that happened ... my wound was minor, but my gang-member friend received treatment at the hospital, and was later released.

The second time a bullet hit me; I was at a private party with friends at the bar where every person had a gun. The fight started over a girl I was with, and the gangster shot me. At the hospital, I said I didn't know who shot me or why it happened, "It was dark, and I was drinking." The bullet didn't go very deep, and it was not very bad.

The police were always watching us, following us, and pulling our car over to search for drugs and weapons. While driving around one day, police pulled us over when we had a lot of cocaine. I was scared because I had a bag that, if found by police, would mean I would be arrested and hauled off to prison. In the US, it's not like Canada, if I was caught with this much dope I would be serving a long sentence. Before the police pulled us over, we bought some burgers and fries at McDonald's, and when I saw them, I was shaking.

There was no insurance on the car, so right away the police were suspicious, having grounds to search us, and the car.

When I think about it now, I smile and laugh, but at that moment, it was terrifying. As soon as I saw the police, I took off the top of the hamburger bun, removed the patties, and put the bag of powder in between the buns, covering it with fries. Then I stuck some more on top and put the paper wrapping around the bundle. When the police came over to the car, I had the 'dope-a-burger' in my hand, and kept eating some fries.

The police searched the car, and then looked through our pockets and shoes. Here I was, standing there with the Cocaine in my hand, disguised inside my burger. The officer said, "Put that down on the hood of the car!" After not finding anything illegal, we were free to go but had to leave the car where it was because there was no insurance. We were lucky that day that no drug-sniffing police dog was there to jump up and bite my hand full of drugs.

When they were finished with us and left, we walked away. My friend, sweat running down his face, asked, "Where're the drugs, what did you do with it?" I looked back at him, put some fries in my mouth, smiled and said, "Don't worry, it's okay, I have it." My everyday life as a gang member and drug dealer involved crazy things happened all the time.

All the neighbours complained and started coming by to check out what was happening. I told them we filed police reports, but they still said they wanted me out, so I stopped paying rent and went back to my friend's place. When I arrived, he said, "What happened. Where is all your money? I hope you didn't bring any guns into my house ... is everything in the car okay?" He laid down strict rules for me living in his home because he had kids and didn't want any trouble, and I agreed not to bring guns, drugs, or anything else into the house. It was more peaceful living there for a while until my gang found another 'crack-shack' for cooking and dealing.

Our gang neighbourhood was like a war zone. One day an enemy gang came in with guns in hand, put down all the people on the floor, and took all the money, drugs and everything else of value, just as my gang had done to them. I was not there at the time ... it happened at night. The constant back and forth revenge and payback between our enemies became an almost weekly event.

We were always able to buy new guns, more drugs, and make money, but the shootings bothered me just as the civil war had in Ethiopia. My gang members didn't want to hear my war stories and anything else I had to say about it. They refused to listen, so I decided on getting out as soon as possible.

Being a gang member means living in fear all the time, watching your back, never having peace in your mind or soul, and never knowing what will happen each day.

When you are ripping off so many people, you never know whom your enemy is. I often asked myself, "Why did I decide to become a gang member?" and "Why had I done such a stupid thing?" I didn't have a clear head at the time I joined, being either drunk or on drugs and I was only now beginning to understand what I had done.

Peter's girlfriend said I could not get out, "Once you are in, it's for life," just like the Mafia. The only escape was to leave town and never come back. I still had my Canadian citizenship and just needed to renew my passport. I kept away from my gang members and did very little until my passport arrived.

I caused so much trouble to my kind friend. The neighbours complained to him about me, but he still helped me after all the danger I put him in. People came to his house, not looking for him, but for me.

Death and Rats

Tim, whom I met when I worked for at a newspaper place, had a wife and four kids. He was African American and became my best friend. We often drank together, and then he started doing hard drugs. We went to a hotel to party for a couple of days, and I told him to go home, but he refused. I left the room to buy some cigarettes, leaving him and a girl there to party.

When I came back, he was on the floor with a needle poked in his arm. The girl was gone. I called 911 and flushed our drugs down the toilet. I never used needles, and it shocked me … seeing my friend dead on the floor. I was so ashamed to see his wife and face her, because their kids would now grow up without a father. I had known him for about six years, and his friends blamed me for his death. What a horrible feeling to know that it was my fault, that my influence had caused his death.

Another friend, Tom, who lived nearby, and hung out with me, didn't come by for a few days. After not seeing him for a while, I went over and peeked in his window. There he was, lying motionless on the floor. After breaking into the house, I stood there wondering what to do. Even though I was still high at the time, this death was too much for me. Crack cocaine was controlling every moment of my life as I stood in the room, smoking more before letting others know about his death.

These two friends, dying from drug overdoses in less than a year, affected me emotionally like never before. Their deaths made me realize that I could end up just like them because of my drug use. I pushed people away from me, knowing they could end up dead too. I didn't want any new friends … preferring to be alone..

A man, who owned a carwash, was okay with me working for him, and I could lay low, hiding from my gang until leaving back to Canada. He let me live in his old, rat-infested mobile home. My wages allowed me to keep buying drugs, and other things I needed to survive.

As loneliness and depression took hold of me, powder cocaine wasn't enough to kill my pain, so I started smoking more crack … my drug of choice. I grew a beard and hid from all my gang member friends. My journey became a trail into oblivion, passing out from drinking and then being taken to the hospital for three days. I couldn't breathe … my mind blacked-out, almost dying three times in Oregon. One doctor in the hospital told me he almost signed my death certificate because I was that close to death. I had become someone else … a person that I didn't know or one that anyone wanted to be around when I was high.

After they released me from the hospital, I went back into my filthy little home for five months, smoking crack with the rats. When I didn't smoke crack, the rats would drive me crazy with their running around. I thought of committing suicide a few times, but I couldn't do it. My worst experience ever was the rats running over me and the crazy noise they would make that kept me awake. Today, when I think back to that scene, I think the rats became addicted to crack as I did. When I ran out, the beady-eyed rodents would scream at me.

I would pray in the mobile, "God if you exist, why am I here? I used to have thousands and thousands of dollars, and now I am here with no money in my pocket, sleeping with crazy rats." When I did think about God, I began to believe I was losing my mind. Talking to my noisy, little friends and not seeing people for a long time drained me. I was paranoid and afraid most of the time when I was not drinking or high. There didn't seem to be an end anytime in sight.

Thankfully, I met a girl while I was living in the mobile home; she befriended me, and invited me to stay at her house for a while. She was a Christian, worked at a bank, and asked me to go to church with her. I said I would drive her there and pick her up after the service was over. She told me every time that when I dropped her off at church, she prayed for me. I told her I wasn't a good person, but she said that was between God and me. While she was with me, she smoked weed even though she knew it was wrong, and against what God wanted for her.

She had a son in his middle teen years. One day he recognized me as a gang member and told me not to get his mom involved in anything I was doing. He knew my history and didn't want to see his mom get hurt, or there was going to be a big problem between us. I decided I needed to distance myself from her after being with her for a short time.

My gang members went to my friends place a few times looking for me and asking where I was. They knew I was Canadian and Ethiopian and they had an idea I may leave soon … searching everywhere. They probably thought I was going to go to the police, tell them all about the gang, and get them in trouble. If they found me, I would not be writing this book right now … I would be dead.

What I hoped would be something good in Oregon, turned into a nightmare, living with rats, thinking about suicide, thinking about everything, running around and around in my mind.

I did go back to Ethiopia to visit my dad once while I lived in Oregon. Peter encouraged me to go before it was too late, and he was right. Dad told me he was glad I came to see him and that he could die in peace now. The time I spent visiting with him was during the day mostly … at night, I'd leave to go drink and party with friends. One week after I returned to Oregon, my dad passed away. That was one of the few, good, memorable things I did … seeing my dad before he died.

Finally, one day there was a knock on my door, my passport had arrived. It took over three months because I made a mistake on the application the first time and had to correct it and wait again to receive it. I didn't want to take a chance getting back into Canada without it … even though I was a citizen; I was not going to risk it.

Chapter 6

Vancouver East Side – Menace and Miracles

When I arrived at the bus depot in Vancouver, I didn't know anyone and had only a few clothes in a small suitcase and about 200 dollars USD that my friend in Oregon had given me. The nearest bar was not far away and quickly became my go-to place of refuge with my money exchanged into Canadian dollars. After having a few beers, I asked a few people about the area and then started hustling.

Vancouver was like no other city I had ever lived in or seen. People were smoking and injecting drugs right out in the open in the Vancouver downtown East Side. I was shocked. It was as if everything was legal, no need to hide your drugs, it was all on every street and alley, like a free society to do anything you wanted without fear of arrest and being thrown in jail.

Living and sleeping under a nearby bridge suited me fine, "Another person was there, so it must be okay," I thought. It looked safe, and I had no worries about someone from my gang hunting me down, seeking revenge. Vancouver was my new home where nobody knew about my past. However, I didn't trust or talk to many people for quite a while. Living outside, looking for a hotel, and just roaming around the streets, helped me feel my way around the area.

The first few days were hard. I could only sleep a few hours in the daytime and then search at night for food and drugs. The Vancouver bus depot was a safe place for washing-up each day. It didn't take very long to learn about the drug culture on the streets and I quickly adapted to being outside on the sidewalks and in alleyways. It's a mean, angry place at times, being aware and on guard was a priority to stay safe and alive.

I stayed at the Salvation Army Belkin house for one month in the winter and then moved back under the bridge to live there during the spring, summer, and fall.

Someone told me about receiving welfare, and shortly after, I had a support check in my hand. While at the office, I met Ail, a person from Somalia. He invited me over to his place and showed me around the city. He lived very close to a place called Union Gospel Mission, (UGM), I didn't tell him where my home was ... under a bridge. His neighbour, Paul, also became my friend and the three of us would hang out together, sharing stories about our life experiences. The UGM mission served free meals to homeless people and anyone else who was hungry, and there were many other places to eat on the East Side at no cost.

Once I felt more at ease being in a new land of freedom, it was easy meeting and getting to know people in Vancouver who were selling drugs and trading stuff on city sidewalks. Vowing not to fall back into my Oregon nightmare, I tried to avoid trouble and anything else that could mess up my life. It was tough, and no matter how hard I searched for answers to my existence, my journey would take twists and unwelcomed turns.

After saving some money and renting a hotel room, I invited a girl over where we partied for two days with no sleep. When she went to use the shared washroom and didn't come back, I went looking for her. There she was, on the floor dead from an overdose, lying on the floor in the hallway. She had not even made it to the bathroom. I went back to my room, and when someone else noticed her, they called 911 … in shock again after seeing another person dead … I felt like death was following me wherever I went.

Death and sickness were all around me in Vancouver. Street people were falling, ambulances screaming in the streets, and police finding addicts dead in doorways. A woman in a liquor store called an ambulance for me one day as I fell sick. As hard as I tried, my memories of living in hell-like conditions were right in front of me most days.

Finding work in Vancouver was not difficult. They hired me right away at a temp-agency. One person drove me around to look for work and found me a job cleaning a ship at night. He picked me up, dropped me off at work each day, and took me home in the morning. However, as soon as I received my pay, it was back on the streets drinking and using … like a plague-filled disease.

I soon began selling drugs for cash to feed my addiction, and this crazy business went on for a while until desperation grabbed hold. I told a few of my friends that I needed to enter a drug rehab program before I went insane or died. I avoided going back to my hotel room, fearing another overdose scene. My paranoid mind made everything so much worse when thinking about it.

"Why was God allowing this nightmare to happen to me," I thought often. I was at the end, and I knew it. "Please help me God," I'm desperate and wanting to die.

After arriving at UGM, and telling them I was a Muslim, they told me that their mission had a Christian recovery program. "Don't be concerned or worry about being a Muslim … just come and try the program. If you don't like it, then you can make your decision to stay or leave," they said.

My mind told me I was not going to make it in their program, but it also whispered that I needed to enter it just to rest and take a break from my life on the streets. It was a warm place to stay, the people were accepting, and the food was filling. "Why not try it … there was nothing to lose," I thought.

After filling out the program application, they told me to come back the next day, "Don't drink or use drugs," they insisted. After not using for only one day, I was shaking with withdrawals and shivering, not able to sleep or function. The waiting was too long, and I drank over the Christmas holidays. When I went back, they asked me what I had been doing. I told them I had only one day clean and sober and they put me in their shelter until December 27, 2005. Finally, my application was reviewed again and they accepted me into the program. What a relief, I now had an opportunity to stay clean and heal … at least I hoped so.

The first three days were scary while detoxing, laying on bunk beds with no sleep, surrounded by others. All my memories flooded my mind, like watching a horror movie repeatedly.

Speaking to my A&D counsellor was impossible at first. I even forgot, at times, how to talk now that I was clean and sober. Our 'one on ones' were short and quiet … returning to my room after our meetings, wondering what was happening or what was next. "Why didn't I want to say anything?" I thought while lying on my bed

Then, one day my counsellor resigned from working at UGM, and I had a new one. It took me a while, but I finally began to open up and talk at my sessions with him.

When thoughts about using overwhelmed me, he would pray for me.

On welfare day, with money in my pocket, I went for a walk by myself in the notorious East Side … a dangerous and risky place to be when trying to stay clean. The entire area around UGM is full of drug users and dealers, which brought back dark thoughts, filling my mind as I walked. All of a sudden, my counsellor walked up to me and asked me to go for a coffee. I was like, "Where did you come from, how did you get here?" If I had not seen him at that very moment, I would have been gone out of the program and back on the streets drinking and using.

I began to open up as we walked and sat down for coffee. Today was a good day for me. My counsellor saved my life. Not long after he rescued me, I began to listen carefully to the teachings of the Bible. Even though I was a Muslim and knew the Quran, I went to a Christian church and wanted to know more of what was in the Bible.

Even though I liked going, standing up and singing, as soon as the pastor began preaching, I fell asleep. People sitting beside me kept waking me up and then moments later, I fell asleep again. For a couple of weeks I kept falling asleep in church. I don't really know why. Maybe because I was still detoxing and unable to sleep at UGM, and then when I felt peace in church, my mind allowed me to sleep.

After church, they gave me an audio cassette, and I listened to it every day. The pastor would visit me every week, go through the Bible with me and pray, and the fear began to disappear. I liked the atmosphere and fellowship, and began to look forward to going to church.

I began to feel different and invited Jesus into my heart. Many people were praying for me. I surrendered my heart, and will to Jesus, at Broadway Church when the pastor asked people to come forward for prayer. I said to myself, "I want to change my life." It wasn't because God delivered me from alcohol and drugs, I wanted to know God in a deeper way; have a closer relationship with Him. I started to go to two churches, Broadway in the morning, and an Ethiopian church in the evening where they spoke my home language.

I had been saved and found myself able to sleep a peaceful night without many nightmares. Because of my Muslim background, it was difficult accepting Jesus as my saviour. I still had so much deep trauma, especially fear and had a hard time trusting people.

I blamed everything on God and questioned whether He even existed. I often thought, "Why did all this happen to me … where were you when I was suffering so much?" I had given up on God a long time ago, but I kept hearing about what Jesus could do. I listened to other people's testimonies and decided to put a little trust and faith in Him, and then wait to see what would happen.

My mind now sober and calm, it was safer to think about things without fear. I was in a better place and able to seek God. I began attending more and more church services. God kept talking to me at these meetings through the messages.

I began to see a much brighter picture and wondered what I was going to do with the rest of my life. I stopped blaming people and God for my past and began to deal with the pain and memories. God lifted me up and removed the weight and burdens that I had carried around with me for so many years. He helped me to focus and be the new man that He wanted me to be. People now cared about me, prayed for me and accepted me unconditionally.

After what seemed like a very long time, thoughts about using began to ease, and my new life of living without drinking was making me happy. Hanging out with sober people and Christians was a new world. I learned slowly with my counsellor's help and began to talk about my childhood, and the military … working through my trauma little by little each day. At the end of each session, my counsellor would pray with me as usual, and I would go for walks to think about things. Over the next four months, I went through a lot of pain before experiencing healing. Learning to control my anger was a process and helped me to deal with people in a new, non-violent way. I stopped lashing out at people as I had done in the past. Also, I attended courses on anger management outside of UGM to help me with my feelings of anger and hate.

Following my graduation from the program, I was baptized in water at the Native Pentecostal church, declaring my faith in Jesus Christ. We discussed what I was dreaming or thinking, and I was mentored on many subjects. I didn't listen to the music of my past, but instead, looked to Bible scriptures on audio recordings ... and hung out with my new Christian brothers and sisters.

My friend Paul found out I was in the UGM program when he came there for meals. I encouraged him to get into the program, but he was not ready for it. We were friends and respected each other's individual decisions, we had to make them for ourselves. After I became an Outreach Worker at UGM, Paul told me he was ready to enter the program. He cleaned up, stayed for one year, but then relapsed back to drugs again. I missed Paul and worried about him being back out on the streets using drugs.

UGM asked me to work, helping with some cleaning at the mission. As I was cleaning the toilets, I would have flashbacks to a time when I had lots of money. The enemy tried to mess with me, but I was a new person in Christ, and I was not ever going back to the former Jemal.

I then worked a maintenance job at UGM for the next six months. The day I received my first cheque, I could see people out my window using drugs. The smells, tastes and thoughts of using rushed back into my mind. I thought about going to cash my cheque, go back, and use. I was shaking and sweating ... it was a terrifying experience. I was frustrated and angry with myself for even thinking about using again. "Why was God allowing me to keep going backwards in my journey?" I thought.

I forced myself to read my Bible ... then dropping to my knees I prayed, asking for God's help. Tears from crying ran down my face as I threw my cheque on the floor. The clock said only 3 pm when I fell asleep. It was as if God knocked me out. When I woke up at midnight, it was too late to cash my cheque. My desire to use was miraculously gone, and sleeping was heaven-like. God's presence was right there with me, a warm, calm, peaceful feeling inside. I had cried out to God from my heart, and He had given me peace and rest.

The next morning I went to the bank, cashed my check and didn't use the money for drugs. My cravings and thoughts about using disappeared, at least for this day. Instead of blowing my paycheck, I gave ten percent to my church, a gift to God.

When I was in the program, I contacted the Christian girl in Oregon that I had been seeing for a while, and she was so happy for me. She wanted to visit me, but I let her know I didn't need any visitors yet. I was in the program and wanted to stay focused on that. Soon after, we stopped connecting, and I never spoke to her again.

After graduating the program, I contacted my ex-wife in the States to file for divorce. A few years later, we both signed the final order and left the past in the past ... not bringing anything of it into my new life.

Chapter 7

Secret Addictions

I moved from living in UGM over to MMP, a small apartment building down the block, managed by the mission. I bought some furniture from the thrift store and settled in as best I could. My new home was a much bigger place to live then what I had before, with a full-size fridge, and stove. The first few days were okay, but soon boredom and depression weighed me down, and sleeping became difficult.

My window-view faced Hastings, one of the noisiest streets in Vancouver with sirens screaming, people yelling and fighting on the sidewalks. Focusing on reading my Bible and praying was near impossible at times.

Before moving, I didn't have problems with sexual addiction, but that changed when I was in this new, strange place that was so much different from where I had been living. At the mission, there were many people all around me every day to hang out with, talk and pray with, but here was different, I was more on my own. I had a computer on my desk, which I didn't know much about yet or how to use very well.

Setting up an email account was not very difficult, but, unbeknownst to me, this would be the beginning journey into shame-filled guilt and confusion. Although I knew going to porn sites was wrong, something pulled me in, especially with nobody around, seeing what was happening. When opening my email, porn 'Pop-Ups' would appear on the screen, dragging me further into temptation.

In the evenings when I returned home from work, the computer was right there in front of me like a hungry beast, pulling at me to go online to feed my addiction. At first, it began as little things when I looked online, and then I looked deeper into the dark, naked web. I was embarrassed, disappointment in myself and stopped reading my Bible or even going to church.

Even though I knew it was wrong in my spirit, I pushed these feelings away. I didn't want to hear or think about how wrong it was. There were two voices talking to me ... my addiction voice and God's voice. We called it the Red Dog and Blue Dog while in the UGM rehab program. One is good versus the other that is evil.

I didn't want to tell anyone about this addiction because everybody looked at me as being clean, not just clean and sober, but spiritually too. People thought I was doing well, but it was far from the truth and reality of my well-being. My relationship with God began to feel dry and distant like I was sliding down into darkness little by little.

I did talk to a counsellor outside of UGM, but it didn't help. He didn't understand what was happening to me and didn't believe in spiritual healing. He told me to get a girlfriend, perhaps it would help me with my addiction; but I didn't want to do that. I already had enough nightmarish memories of suffering from failed marriages and crazy girlfriends.

Being alone in my apartment online, in control of not having to be accountable to a woman was fine with me, no need to meet in person. This was the nature of my addiction. It consumed my rational thinking and actions, twisting into believable lies from the enemy.

Finally, after being on the computer for hours one evening, I opened my Bible to 1 John 2:15-17 where Jesus talked about not loving and not having the Father's love. Without His love, you fall into loving the things of the world, including drug cravings and physical pleasure.

1 John 1:5-9, This is the message which we have heard from Him and declare to you, that God is light and in Him is no darkness at all. If we say that we have fellowship with Him, and walk in darkness, we lie and do not practice the truth. But if we walk in the light as He is in the light, we have fellowship with one another, and the blood of Jesus Christ His Son cleanses us from all sin. If we say that we have no sin, we deceive ourselves, and the

truth is not in us. If we confess our sins, He is faithful and just to forgive us our sins and to cleanse us from all unrighteousness.

When I read that, I thought about what Jesus said and started praying, asking Him for help. Then I opened my Bible to Psalm 51 where David cried out to God:

"Have mercy on me, O God, according to your unfailing love; according to your great compassion. Blot out my transgressions. Wash away all my iniquity and cleanse me from my sin, for I know my transgressions, and my sin is always before me. Against you, you only, have I sinned and done what is evil in your sight, so you are right in your verdict and justified when you judge. Surely, I was sinful at birth, sinful from the time my mother conceived me. Yet you desired faithfulness even in the womb; you taught me wisdom in that secret place. Cleanse me with hyssop, and I will be washed, and I will be whiter than snow. Let me hear joy and gladness; let the bones you have crushed rejoice. Hide your face from my sins and blot out all my iniquity."

Tears poured down my face as I kept praying, asking God for His forgiveness. I told God that if He was willing to work with me, I was ready to yield my will to His.

I continued to pray, "Create in me a pure heart, O God, and renew a steadfast spirit within me. Do not cast me from your presence or take your Holy Spirit from me.

Restore unto me the joy of your salvation and grant me a willing spirit, to sustain me."

I wanted to be free of sin and able to help others with their past trauma, pain, and addictions, including sexual addiction. It all began to make sense to me, and I prayed again as David in the Bible did:

"Then I will teach transgressors your ways so that sinners will turn back to you. Deliver me from the guilt of bloodshed, O God, you who are God my Saviour, and my tongue will sing of your righteousness. Open my lips, Lord, and my mouth will declare your praise."

A warm peace came over my mind, heart and soul, falling asleep until waking up at 2 am. Although I felt strong, my computer was still there, right in front of me. It was something I didn't want to see whenever I woke up or walked in the door. When I think about it now, my computer was the door to sexual addiction ... right there ready for me to sit down and surf the web every moment I was in the room with it. Looking at the screen was a continual struggle for me, the same as if there was crack cocaine sitting there on the table for me to try and resist.

When I visited my outside counsellor, he didn't get it. We just couldn't agree on anything in the spiritual realm. I remember being in his office, telling him, "I can't sleep anymore ... I feel shame and guilt as if I'm hiding something from God." Then, when I began to cry, he told me that he understood what was upsetting me and because

I was in a spiritual relationship, I didn't need him for help. "Maybe you are too sick," he said. What a thing to say to me! That was the last time I saw him and continued to pray: "Create in me a pure heart, O God, and renew a steadfast spirit within me."

Was I healed and cured 100% of this secret addiction? Of course not, but God was working on it with me. For a few weeks, I was okay with my computer still being in my room, but I knew inside that it had to go. I was in a battle, unseen by the eye, but I could feel it in my spirit. I look at this as being similar to when I fought in the Ethiopian war.

When I fought in the physical war, I had to have all my gear and weapons with me at all times. The same goes for spiritual warfare. With my computer in my house, the enemy was right there in front of me, tempting me. Unlike fighting with a gun in my hand, I used a sword … the sword of the Spirit and God's Word. His words in the Bible are packed and backed up with the Spirit of God.

At times, lust led me to believe that it is good, fun and exciting; whereas when we awake to God's love, we discover we have been sleeping with the enemy in the room.

2 Corinthians 10:3-6: "For though we walk in the flesh, we do not war according to the flesh. For the weapons of our warfare are not carnal but mighty in God for pulling down strongholds, casting down arguments and every high thing

that exalts itself against the knowledge of God, bringing every thought into captivity to the obedience of Christ, and being ready to punish all disobedience when your obedience is fulfilled. (NKJV).

Finally, I looked out my window to make sure nobody was below and out it went, smashing on the sidewalk. As soon as it went out the window, the evil spirits went with it, leaving my room a clean place for me to live and grow in God's love.

I was stronger again and started telling my Christian friends and pastor about my computer, sexual addiction and what had happened. The Holy Spirit gave me serenity, and I asked friends to come to my room and pray with me.

Living with shame and guilt for so long was horrible and robbed me of so many things. It was a secret that I kept to myself, my struggles hidden. I was agonizing on the inside and going through the motions on the outside of going to church, reading my Bible, or at least trying to. I felt like a hypocrite, grieving deeply inside my heart for what I was doing. So many times, I asked myself, "Why can't I stop doing this?"

Unlike my outside counsellor, the Bible had the answer: Romans 7:15-20, "I do not understand what I do. For what I want to do I do not do, but what I hate I do. And if I do what I do not want to do, I agree that the law is good. As it is, it is no longer I myself who do it, but it is sin living in me. For I know that good itself does not dwell in me, that is, in my sinful nature. For I have the desire to do what is good, but I cannot carry it out. For I do not do the good I want to do, but the evil I do not want to do—this I keep on doing. Now if I do what I do not want to do, it is no longer I who do it, but it is sin living in me that does it."

God was fighting the war of pain with me this time. He was there to help me, but I had to do the work, with His strength and guidance. I just kept calling to God for help, to give me the strength that I needed to free myself from these sinful behaviours.

It was hard at times, for me to understand what caused me to seek out sexual things on the internet. Perhaps my pain from my childhood times, feelings of being alone, unloved or abused by the military had something to do with it. More often than not, I struggled with feelings of isolation, and abandonment, and couldn't experience my true feelings. My behaviours became a simple solution to disconnect from my trauma, using negative sexual dissatisfaction to help numb, block, and detach from my painful past emotions.

My mind was searching for someone or something to love me when I was distant from God and felt no love. Pornography had become my go-to choice for comfort and pleasure that released euphoric chemicals into my brain. Just like when I used cocaine and had to do more and more to feel the high … this addiction was similar. As my mind became bored with what I was looking at, I looked deeper to get the same effect at things that were more explicit. I became a prisoner as my shame and guilt tightened around my heart. My soul was at war with my behaviours that contradicted my beliefs and values.

On the outside, I appeared to behave well with my peers and friends, but on the inside, I was screaming. I pretended that nothing was wrong and tried to act like my spiritual life was good.

I was in a battle for my life. Ephesians 6:12: "For we wrestle not against flesh and blood, but against principalities, against powers, against the rulers of the darkness of this world, against spiritual wickedness in high places" By going on the internet to look at porn, I had separated myself from God and yielded myself to wicked, spiritual powers and hosts."

As a Christian, I now arm myself for defence in battle with the sword of the Spirit, which is the word of God. It subdues and removes evil desires and thoughts when they come to my mind. A single scripture is all I need at times, to remove the temptations. A vain heart will be vain in prayer, so I pray with all kinds of prayer, public, private, and secret ... social and solitary. I pray with all the parts of prayer ... confession of sin, petition for mercy, and thanksgiving for mercy received. I do it by the grace of God and the Holy Spirit, in dependence on, and according to, His will and teaching.

Because of guilt and shame that I felt it was hard to talk about this dark addiction. Guilt stemmed from what I did, and shame was about who I had become … with feelings that I was broken, damaged, worthless, and a bad person. I hid my guilt and nakedness for a long time until recently. Adam from Genesis in the Bible experienced the first case of shame, and humankind has followed ever since his fall.

Genesis 3:10 "He (Adam) answered, I heard you (God) in the garden, and I was afraid because I was naked; so I hid."

Now, with this addiction behind me, having made enormous progress in my recovery, I have a desire to help others with their painful secrets. A lot of men and women, who are Christians, and addicts in recovery, are struggling with compulsive behaviours, and they are doing it alone. We all need others in our lives with whom we can be open and honest, self-revealing so that we don't fall into the enemy's weapons of fear that he uses against us. Worry, anxiety, and fear can overwhelm us into darkness, controlling our decisions.

"Do not be anxious about anything, but in every situation, by prayer and petition, with thanksgiving, present your requests to God. And the peace of God, which transcends all understanding, will guard your hearts and your minds in Christ Jesus." - Philippians 4:6-7.

Now, moving forward, I want to help others more than ever. I kept my secret hidden inside me for a long time. I have felt their pain and loneliness. I know how secrets affect spiritual progress. I pray that by telling my story in this book, it will motivate others to feel that it's okay to talk about this shame-filled subject. We don't have to feel this guilt anymore. We can be free from the sin that drags us down into confusion and distress.

It's important for people in recovery to talk about all their addictions or they will continue to carry them with them, feeling even more shame and guilt, eventually relapsing and giving in to their addictions. I went through it … God forgave me, and I am a new person now with all that mess behind me.

I used to be afraid of what people would think about me, but now, if I am going to help others, I need and want to talk about it. When my wife first read the draft copy of this chapter, she was shocked! She knew some of my past, but not as much as I have told here. She didn't ask me about the details, and I didn't tell her. However, before I let her read this chapter, I talked to her about it and let her know that she didn't know the whole story … just to prepare ahead of time for the shock she was about to receive. Yes, she was shocked, very shocked.

However, after reading it, she said, "Jemal that was the old you … the past is the past. This is not who you are now. God has transformed you into the man I know and love." My wife trusts God, and she trusts me, that is what is important in our relationship with each other.

Whilst preparing the previous chapters, I was thinking about this one a lot … it was on my mind every day. Someday my children, grandchildren, relatives, and close friends will likely read this. "Is it worth it?" I thought. The thing for me was to show how powerful God is, to give Him the glory for my deliverance from this sin. It's okay for my kids to know what I struggled with before I became a man of God, serving people. At least when people read about this, it might help them think about and acknowledge their problems instead of pushing them down and keeping them a secret. God already knows all about this and still loves us.

For me, I came from Africa, and it's a deep shame to admit to or talk about sexual addiction. Growing up as a Muslim makes this issue a taboo. I buried this for a long time. Talking about my alcohol and drug addiction was simple, but not sexual addiction.

This addiction was harder to deal with and overcome, especially when I had worked so hard to buried it.. It is not like drugs or alcohol addiction. It is very sticky and stuck to me like gum on a sidewalk. When you quit drugs, it's not in front of you all the time, but when you walk down the street, reminders of your sexual addiction are everywhere around you.

When I first gave my life to Christ, as a new believer, the Bible said, "When you come to Jesus, you are a new person … all former things pass away." I was happy then, felt stronger, and no fear about talking to people about

Jesus. However, when I fell back into sexual addiction, everything began to break down again… I had no strength or enough joy to talk about God with other people. My inspiration was gone as if everything inside me was dead.

When they asked me to be an outreach worker, I didn't tell the manager about what I was struggling with …, "How am I going to tell him about that?" I thought. "How am I going to talk to people, pray with them about their troubles when I'm living with this sickness?" I couldn't help people be free if I was in chains to my addiction. That is why I refused to work as an outreach worker at the time. I said, "Thank you for offering me this position with UGM, but I'm not ready … when I'm ready, I'll tell you."

Complete Deliverance

After battling this addiction for so long, I said to myself, "I need to get away from down here in the noisy East Side and spend time with God." The only place I knew of that was spiritually quiet, was at Rivendell on Bowen Island. I had been there before, doing my Step 5. I had received my baptism in the Holy Spirit at Rivendell … a place where God walked and talked with me.

I went there for a few days to fast, read my bible and pray. I did believe that God had already forgiven me, but I didn't feel completely free yet. One day I was outside, standing where the chapel is now, screaming at God, "Are you listening to me ... give me my joy back. I can't live like this anymore ... please, I'm begging you..."   I looked up at the trees and saw one shaking, the wind whistling through the branches. I thought, "What's going on?" Then something came over me, and my nightmare was gone. The heaviness I had been carrying around had been lifted. Suddenly the wind stopped, and the tree stopped shaking. I turned around and saw a person standing near me, so I asked him, "Did you see the wind and tree shaking?" "No, I didn't see any wind or anything," he replied. I didn't want to ask him more questions because he might have thought I was crazy. It was on my third day at Rivendell, and I just said, "Thank you God for showing me that vision." He gave me this scripture:

Ezekiel 36:25-27:

"I will sprinkle clean water on you, and you will be clean; I will cleanse you from all your impurities and from all your idols. I will give you a new heart and put a new spirit in you; I will remove from you your heart of stone and give you a heart of flesh. And I will put my Spirit in you and move you to follow my decrees and be careful to keep my laws."

It was now time for me to go back inside the lodge, pack my things and go home. I felt like a different person … thoroughly changed in mind, heart, and soul. God had given me my joy back along with His Holy Spirit. I had never felt this before because of the shame and guilt that I could not shake. I slept much better after leaving Rivendell … without dreaming anymore about this addiction to the internet. I knew without a doubt that all this was behind me, and I would now be free to spread the good news about Jesus.

I began talking about sexual addiction in groups which helped others to start their journey to freedom. I give God all the glory and praise for my deliverance.

Chapter 8

A Life Truly Worth Living Indeed

In 2006, I met a woman, Vincia, at Broadway Church when we were both taking a spiritual, 'Life worth Living' course. I had not been attending this church very long and had recently divorced, not looking to get into another relationship anytime soon. When I glanced over to where she was sitting, my face widened with a smile, and I remember thinking, "Wow, this lady is special, maybe I will get to know and talk to her."

It was a happy day for me, looking back and forth at each other during this class. We didn't talk while we were at the church that day, and I didn't see her for a while. Of course, I thought about her every day and prayed that I would meet her again so we could talk.

Vincia went on a cruise for two weeks, and when she returned to Vancouver, she saw that I noticed her absence. I asked her what she did on her days off, and she replied that she was a nurse, working twelve hour shifts, and she slept. She said, "Yes," when I asked her if I could take her out to dinner … only as a friend. We went for coffee downtown, and she saw the way I was looking at her, smiling, with a look of wonder on my face. We continued to go out together as friends for a while, enjoying each other's company, talking about many things that came to mind. We didn't always agree with each other on every subject, but I felt that it's important to be open and honest, not holding back.

One day when we were downtown, we began arguing. She was angry and upset at me. The next time we met, she was surprised when I forgave her, and the matter was never discussed again. She asked me to give her some time to deal with the issues that she had from her own past. She had been reading a book and felt God telling her that she wanted me to be perfect. She just needed time, giving me a chance to show her the true nature of this new man in her life.. A trip to visit my brother in Germany was perfect timing, giving Vincia space … and time to think and pray.

Soon after I returned home, we started dating … a step forward from just being friends. My divorce was final, and I felt free to be in another relationship.

I began opening up to her, sharing my past life. I wanted to share with her everything that I could, in the hopes that we would marry one day. I wanted her to feel comfortable with me; and our life together, and the only way to do that was for her to know me, the old me as well as the new me. Like most people in a new relationship, we were somewhat nervous, but as time passed, we began sharing our feelings, smiles and laughs.

Before asking her to marry me I needed to ask her father for his permission and phoned her sister so that I could speak to her dad. After he gave me his blessing, I prayed about it and got the answer that this was the woman for me. I put my trust in God for His new plan for my life, he changed my heart. God heard me and gave me a deep peace in my spirit, a warm feeling with no anxiety or stress in my mind.

Vincia thought we weren't in a serious relationship yet, and not at the marriage stage. However, it happened very quickly. When I proposed to her in October, after a few months of dating, she asked me for a yearlong engagement so that we could get to know each other better before getting married. We read many books together and prepared for the marriage ceremony that was one year away.

I had saved money for an engagement ring, but when the store clerk swiped my bank card to complete the purchase, I was stunned … not enough money in my account. We tried again with the same result. "Why wasn't this working, why was my bank account empty?" I thought. Confused and upset, off to the bank I went to ask what happened.

The bank informed me there was money owing to them from a fifteen-year-old debt, and that the funds I had on deposit had been seized to pay them back. A sick feeling overwhelmed me for a few minutes until I realized this was not the end of the world ... there was a solution, just start saving all over again until there was enough to buy Vincia her engagement ring.

The day I proposed, I was very nervous ... not calm as usual. After we drove Vincia's friend to the Sky Train, I could tell she was sensing that something was different with me. I asked her to marry me that day in her apartment ... the way she wanted it done, privately, and of course I respected her wishes. That day when I knelt down in front of her, she was quiet. We had only been dating for three and a half months, and she was surprised when I asked.

I looked up and said, "You have to say something, I'm still kneeling here ... say yes or no." She looked down at me, smiled, and said, "Yes." It was an incredible day for me, and a true blessing from God.

We both attended pre-marital counselling with my UGM counsellor and friend, Kumar, who knew my full story, everything about me that I shared with him in the program and after graduating. Vincia felt comfortable with Kumar, a kind, gentle, Christian man who didn't judge. He encouraged her to ask God for what she specifically wanted in a man.

"If you're not specific, you can't complain after," he said with a grin.

She asked God for someone who was gentle, someone who loved God, and someone who will cook for her. Before we were married, she came to see me when I was volunteering at church. She saw that I was not doing it to find a wife, and knew my faith in God was real. I was not doing it to impress others and find a wife as I saw others doing.

During counselling sessions, we learned about the importance of having good communication skills when we talked about financial stuff. It's challenging and feels awkward when you are single and want to tell someone how much money you make or what you do with your money.

Counselling helped us deal with many things even if we felt uncomfortable about it. Kumar asked me if I didn't mind making less money than my wife did. I said, "No, I don't mind if she makes more than me." He told me most men don't like it when their wife makes more than them. It was good receiving counselling to learn all these things and deal with it before we were married, not after.

During the winter of our engagement, I didn't see her for a while because she was working so much. One night my car was not able to drive in the snow, so I began walking to her place to see her after she finished her day shift. I was freezing because I had to walk a long way in the cold. She wasn't home when I arrived, so I waited outside, shivering. When she arrived at the apartment, she found me on a bench. When I told her I had walked from downtown, she smiled, saying, "It was so sweet of you to come see me in such cold weather."

After I left her place, heading home, I fell in the snow so many times. Even though it was cold, I didn't care … I was in love, and you do things like that when you are in love.

The first time Vincia let me drive her car, I parked it in front of her place, but when we went down, it was gone …. A tow truck hauled it away. She had never gotten a ticket with that car before. After calling to find the vehicle at the tow truck yard, we took a bus, she didn't talk to me all the way there. Our engagement was a year of testing and helped us get to know each other and see what life was going to be like together once we were married.

She introduced me to one of her brothers, and we went out for dinner together. It was important for her to feel and know her brother's impression of me. Soon after, I met her sister at church and soon knew all her family members.

For me, and many others, I had a need to feel loved and accepted for who I was. There was not much love seen or felt during most of my life, not back in Ethiopia, nor in the US and Canada before going to UGM. Once I developed my trust in Kumar, he became my surrogate dad, someone I trusted.

During our engagement, Kumar suggested we go to a spiritual retreat on Bowen Island to talk and pray together about our relationship. He wanted us to see and feel what it would be like to be married. We were able to get away from the noisy city and stay on top of a mountain in a beautiful place. At first, it was challenging but turned into a wonderful time with great memories.

Before my wedding, I went to my bachelor party at a park up in BC's interior. A few of us headed over to the river for a swim. My friend, Fari, jumped into the cold water first, and then two more followed him. I jumped in and did the backstroke … not looking ahead to where I was swimming. Where we plunged into the water it was calm, but off to the edge, it was running faster, and we could see rocks poking up through the waves.

I loved to swim and was having a good time until I heard Fari yelling at me, "Jemal, watch out," as I entered the fast water, going downstream into the rocks. My strap-on sandals flew off my feet as I struggled in the rapids, hearing my friends yelling at me from shore. A young kid had been standing by the edge, and Fari yelled, "Throw him your board, throw him your board," and the kid yelled back, "No," followed by Fari, "C'mon, throw him the board."

Thank God I didn't hit my head on a rock as I splashed around in the fast-moving current. After rolling around for a while in the bubbles and waves, I was able to swim to the edge and climb out. I thank God that my fiancé, Vincia, wasn't there, standing on the shore feeling helpless as she watched her husband-to-be thrashing about in the water. Even when she heard what nearly happened to me, it was quite upsetting for her. Vincia and I were married in October at the Broadway Church. I was on a journey, and God was leading me this time.

When Vincia and I got married, I felt a sense of peace and acceptance. The moment, I said, "I do," I now had new family members. I gained a completely new family. I had lost my parents and now I had the opportunity to form a relationship with her parents. I was without my family for so long, and now my heart filled with joy.

When we arrived at the airport to leave Canada for our honeymoon, they told me that I couldn't go to the Caribbean through the States. It was due to a previous charge against me, and I asked if there was something they could do ... make an exception perhaps.

After waiting six hours, they told us that we definitely couldn't transfer planes in the States and that we had to wait until the next day to buy a new ticket that avoided the stopover. After praying about it, we purchased another plane fare and went on our honeymoon. We found out later that the airline gave us credit back for that first plane ticket that we hadn't been able to use; we were able to use it to go to Africa the following year.

After our honeymoon, I moved into my wife's apartment. It took a couple of weeks to feel comfortable in my new home. We talked and prayed about it, then painted the rooms a new colour, bought a new sofa, and it started to feel like home for the next two years.

My wife learned many new things about me after we were married. Like how I unpacked my suitcase, dumping everything out onto the floor in front of the laundry machine, leaving it in a messy pile. Unlike me, my wife took them out when she was ready to wash them. The most difficult thing for her was dealing with the nightmares I had at times. She saw and heard me yelling and punching the air while sleeping. During these nightmare episodes, she would shake me hard to wake me up. My nightmares are less frequent now, but it does put a strain on our relationship from time to time when these traumatic dreams happen.

A year later, we went to Ethiopia, visiting with my family and seeing the country where I had grown up. It was so very different from where Vincia was born and raised in the Caribbean and Canada. Also, of course, it was good for me to see my family again in Africa after so many years away. They asked me if I was still a Christian, and although one of them was still not happy with it, they welcomed both of us with open arms.

We spent some time with my Christian aunt in Ethiopia and went to church together. Other than my wife and me, she is the only Christian in my family. I remember a long time ago when she first became a Christian. My family would not talk to her for a long time. She had a strong faith in Christ and encouraged me that our other relatives would become Christians too one day.

I told them my story about recovering from addiction in Vancouver, but they thought I was using this as an excuse to be a Christian. They learned how we helped people at UGM, and how much I had changed for the better. Before we left and departed back to Canada, they said they were happy for me and that I was walking the right path.

It was different going to a Christian church in Ethiopia. All the people dressed in white removed the distractions that we sometimes have here in Canada when looking around to see what everyone is wearing. Everyone dressing the same made it much easier to focus on God. We enjoyed our time in Ethiopia, our life together unfolding into union blessed by God.

A Blessing - Our Son is Born

After arriving back home, we often prayed about having children. I also wanted and prayed about becoming an ordained minister. Other pastors would ask me, "Why do you want to be ordained?" I told them, "I think God wants me to so that I can help more people." Even my wife asked me why. I knew that some people didn't want to go to a pastor they don't know and trust and ask them to perform their marriage ceremony. Many people I knew down in the East Side were close to me, and I wanted to help them any way I could.

After being ordained in Alberta, people began asking me to pray for them and perform their marriage ceremony.

It's not about the position of being a minister … it's about connecting to a community where people ask me to help them with their lives. Working as a minister in a church as a Pastor was not my goal or intent. I preferred working in the downtown East Side, where I could preach God's word and encourage people to have hope and faith.

Soon after being ordained, we found out that my wife was pregnant. We had watched all of our friends have children, and now, after praying and trusting God, we were going to be blessed with a child of our own, raising them in a Christian home. A few months later, we decided to sell our condominium and moved outside of Vancouver. We were six months into my wife's pregnancy when we bought our new home, furnished it, and prepared for our baby. The time flew by so quickly, and we liked the new area we chose to live at in Coquitlam. We ate a lot too, especially with my wife being pregnant. I would call her and ask what she wanted to eat, pick it up, and we enjoyed gaining weight together.

Then, one evening my wife called me to pick her up at home and take her to the hospital. Our neighbours asked her if everything was okay as she waited out front for me to arrive. They asked if they should take her to the hospital, but she wouldn't go without me. I picked her up and arrived at the hospital where we were sent back home to wait.

Later that night she woke me up and said she was in labour. I said, "Don't worry, I'm praying for you," and went back to sleep. She walked up and down all night and at 5 am, woke me up again and said she needed to go to the hospital right away. Her contractions were close together. I got up out of bed, showered, shaved,not at all concerned or in a hurry. But my wife was not calm, quite the opposite.

"Jemal, we need to go … right now! I have everything packed and ready at the door," she said. It seemed she was in a panic of sorts, but I still puttered around, taking my time.

I told her I wanted to have something to eat and made a delicious smoothie. My wife said again, "Jemal, we have to go now, not after you have something to eat." When we got in the car, I asked her if she wanted me to drive safe or fast. My wife responded with, "Just get me there fast … I don't care how you drive."

When we arrived at the hospital, we had to wait until staff admitted Vincia. I didn't think it would take very long, but it seemed like forever. During the labour, I didn't know what to do and called her sister Melissa, to come and help support my wife during the delivery. When my wife saw me holding our baby for the first time, she smiled, seeing my son and me together. I called many people to see Adam and sent many pictures to people on our phones. When it was time to take Adam home I drove so slowly that my wife said:

"Jemal, you need to go faster. People are walking faster than we are. You're going too slow, like driving in a school zone."

During the first year, Adam, like many other newborn babies, was not a very good sleeper. My wife and I had very little sleep, and it strained and tested our relationship. We were tired from having to wake up at all hours of the night to care for Adam. It was the first time we had argued or fought in our marriage because we were just so exhausted..

My wife started to get depressed and felt lonely after having Adam. He would cry for long periods at a time, and it didn't matter what we did for him, you just had to wait it out. She struggled for months alone not telling anyone, not even me. In hindsight, she wished she had reached out to someone because the outcome for situations like this can be deadly.

Vincia told me she was too embarrassed to tell anyone for a long time, thinking that she was weak and couldn't handle motherhood. Sometimes she couldn't even pray, all she could do was listen to Bible verses for strength to help her through the day. Isaiah 26:3, "You will keep in perfect peace those whose minds are steadfast because they trust in you." Day by day, God brought her through her struggle, and her walk with God deepened. I wished I could have helped Vincia with her painful struggles. Micah 7:8, "Do not gloat over me, my enemy! Though I have fallen, I will rise. Though I sit in darkness, the Lord will be my light."

James 5:14-15, "Is anyone among you sick? Let them call the elders of the church to pray over them and anoint them with oil in the name of the Lord. And the prayer offered in faith will make the sick person well; the Lord will raise them up. If they have sinned, they will be forgiven."

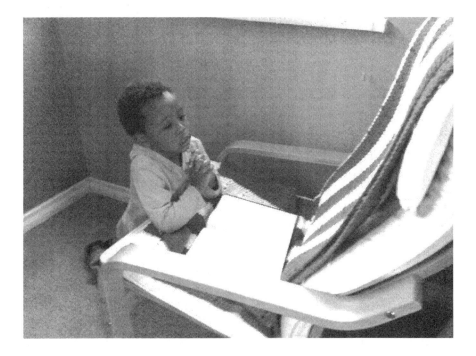

"Train up a child in the way he should go, and when he is old, he will not depart from it." Proverbs 22:6

Adam helping to prepare food bags for homeless

Dad and Sister

At home in Ethiopia with my family - 2010

Adam with his Grampa George

Vincia's mom Celistina: my second mom

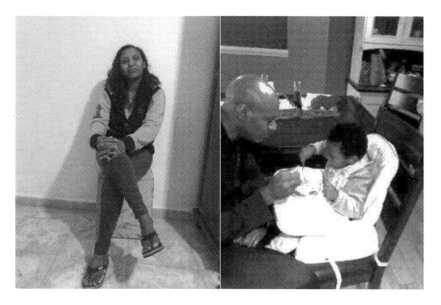

My sister Lububa - Oatmeal together with Adam

UGM Graduation Day – Previous home under bridge

My brother Abraham and I – I am the one sitting

Adam with his cousins

Jemal holding Adam – one day old

Vincia and Adam   Teaching Adam to Cook

Family time together in Vancouver

Chapter 9

Working With Jesus

After graduating from the drug rehab program, I worked as a maintenance person at UGM. It was part-time, five days a week, four hours each day, cleaning toilets, fixing doors, painting, and doing other things around the mission. While looking out the windows during this four-month internship program, I saw people using and had thoughts about drugs and alcohol.

Not that I was overwhelmed or tempted in my mind to use, but when seeing it … the crack and meth pipes, people exhaling clouds of smoke, I would sometimes have a taste in my mouth. The memories in my brain triggered my imagination to feelings, smells and, actually tasting the drug for a few seconds. Going downtown after work was even worse, there was nothing left to my imagination, it was right there, all around me.

One day, a street ministry person whom I was working with down near Main and Hastings, brought me into an alley on Hastings, one-half block west of Main Street. She had an eight-passenger minivan, checking on people and praying for them. When she asked me for help, I said, "okay," not knowing what I was getting myself into at the time.

She also went down there to take people to church and parked the van near the alley, a horrible place that smelled of urine and other nasty stuff. It was welfare day. I had been down around there when I was using, but it felt much different this day ... the filth, rank odours, and seeing addicts pushing needles into their veins gave me a headache, a sick feeling in my stomach until I vomited. I was only six months clean and sober, and this was far too much for me to stay there, watching and feeling such pain and suffering.

She said, "What's wrong with you, just pray in the name of Jesus." I replied, "No, no, no, I can't do this," and ran out of the alley, up the street back to UGM. As soon as I arrived, I started vomiting again. I talked to the counsellor and a few other people there, and said, "I'm feeling better now, but I'm not going back to the downtown East Side ... not for a long time." Perhaps if I stayed close to the area around the mission, I could avoid such things, stay safe. Although my room at UGM had a window facing the street where I could see people selling drugs, I did feel safer, and my stomach wasn't heaving as it had been.

After that horrible experience, I would go to meetings and elsewhere by avoiding that area as often as possible, but the devil kept attacking and tempting me. I was standing on Hastings one day and saw a person with crack in his hand. My mind just went off to using right away. I wanted to walk over and buy some, thinking, "Just a little bit … just to try it again. I had money in my pocket, so why not, just a bit wouldn't hurt." What a crazy moment this was, "How could I be so stupid to think such a thing," I thought to myself.

But I was lucky this time because my counsellor, Kumar, came by and said, "What are you doing?" I was standing there with money in my hand … ready to buy. I said, "Umm, I don't know, where are you going, Kumar?" He replied, "I'm going to UGM."

"Well, I'm going with you," and walked back with him. I laugh at it now, but it wasn't funny at the time.

I was honest with Kumar and told him what happened, what I was thinking. I was still working part-time at UGM as a maintenance worker, and not ready to work full time yet. I still had to be stronger and patient. For the next six months, I continued to work from 8 am to noon, knowing that overworking myself would lead to stress and tiredness, which could very well lead to a relapse in my recovery. When an opening to work at UGM's Thrift Store came up, I applied, and they hired me, full time. My duties were working as a 'swamper' on the truck they used to deliver and pick up furniture, along with the clothes and other stuff that they sold in the store. While working maintenance, I was tempted to use drugs and have women many times, but now I was stronger. It was a full-time job, Monday to Friday, 9 am to 5 pm. In the morning, we delivered furniture, and in the afternoon, we picked stuff up, having a set schedule for each community. It was back when UGM only had their mission at the corner of Princess and Cordova Street.

Now, the old building is for women and the new building for men only. When I was in the program at the old building, we had about thirty men, housed in rooms with three bunk beds ... six people in each room and it took quite a while before we moved into our separate space. Living with six people in the same place was hard. There was not much room and very tight quarters. There were many conflicts, loud snoring and a high turnover of people leaving.

Outreach

When I started working as an 'Outreach Worker' in the old building, they trained me as a ministry support worker. After we served lunch to the homeless people and residents in the rehab program, we went out into the city and reached out to people in need. We walked around the East Side streets and in the alleyways, two of us would walk together, and it didn't bother me as it did before. I had nearly two years clean, more stable and grounded in my faith. On occasion, I still had brief thoughts of my past. However, I had a girlfriend now, goals that are more positive and hopes for a fulfilled, happy future.

While I was praying with a group of workers for God to send me a friend I could trust and share my questions and thoughts with, in walked a man, and I asked God, "Is this the one?" Like me, Fari was a Muslim until he arrived in Canada and gave his life to Christ. We connected very fast and had so many things in common, we hit it off right away, and are still the best of friends today. He arrived here from war-torn Iran, and although he was not a child soldier like me, he knew what it was like to be surrounded by violence. We hung around together so much that people would get our names mixed up. Our relationship was so close that Fari was the best man at my wedding.

Our mutual love for Christ drew us together like brothers with a spiritual connection. The street walks we went on were an adventure for us. We loved going into the alleyways, meeting and talking to people on the East Side. It was intense at times, but this is what we liked to do together. We felt called by God and accepted people right where they were, in whatever position their lives were currently at.

We encouraged each other as we grew in our faith and began preaching God's word. Neither of us held back, nor were we embarrassed about our faith in Christ. We preached the gospel wherever we went, showing people compassion and love. We were both ordained around the same time and had wives and children. Looking back, I know God put us in each other's path to strengthen each other and help us both in our journey of friendship and faith … far beyond just being co-workers at the mission.

Down in the East Side alleys, I gave people my business card after talking to them about housing, food, and the UGM program. We did this two to three hours, twice a week, sometimes three times a week if we were not too busy with the mission. Once we moved over to the new building, the outreach ministry on the street continued, as it still does today. I liked the old building … the relationships were much closer and personal, it felt more closely connected. We were able to see and visit with all the program residents every day no matter where they were.

As an outreach worker today, I focus on people still living out on the streets, not those already in the rehab program. I help people get into the program and place them in Gateway … a place where they can rest whilst waiting for a space in the program. Not all people who are in Gateway enter the UGM rehab program. We help them find a place in the community that will best suit their needs for recovery.

Christmas, Easter, and Thanksgiving at the mission is always a special time, working together with hundreds of volunteers when we feed thousands of people. In the summer, UGM puts on a BBQ for the entire community and all are welcome. The Christmas holidays are always a welcomed time at the mission for my family and I. For a couple of years, we've joined the festivities in the drop-in centre with the residents and staff. Many people don't have a family to be with, some simply don't have family nearby, whereas others have no family at all. Once people are gathered and sat down, I would walk up to the pulpit and begin preaching about how this was a holy day, hoping to bring a Christian atmosphere into the room. Even though there was laughter and talking, I continued with His word.

For the most part, people were smiling, laughing and talking to each other, hugging and 'Merry Christmas' wishes followed by more hugs and smiles. Some residents had only been at UGM for a few days and looked sad, missing their families and friends, eyes gazed down at the floor. When the singers began, you could see and feel God's presence begin to change the sadness. Many of the residents and guests didn't know what to expect, and neither did I.

Every person who attends this function receives at least one gift wrapped up in colourful paper and bows. Early Christmas morning, a band sets up their instruments and microphones to sing carols. Some people from outside the mission joined in; especially devoted volunteers. Once things settled down, a staff member goes to the pulpit and announces a Christian trivia contest. The person who gets the right answer receives an extra gift on the table. We try to have as many people as possible involved in the fun.

Last year I brought my ball of energy son and wife. Adam was so excited when he opened his gift that was a hockey game to play with on the floor. Once people knelt down on the floor to play with him, the room began to feel like an intimate family gathering. As they were playing together, we gave more gifts to the residents, beginning with those who had the longest clean and sober time. It started with about fifteen years, slowly moving down to the number of days. Eventually, everyone was getting up to receive gifts. The music and singing increased, and I could see and feel God's presence, a warm presence that changes lives.

Today, when I see people using drugs around UGM or downtown, I still remember the feeling of what it was like being homeless, lonely, confused and a foggy mind when high. Now it is much easier to make the right choice. I have dealt with much of the pain from my past, and I know drugs do not have to be in my life anymore. I like my new life. I avoid places and people, if or when memories bother me too much.

What helped and inspired me was seeing and talking to the UGM Alumni … they had years of clean time, and their lives were in order according to God's plan. They had their family members back in their life, some now married. Their new life, how they have changed, inspires me, gives me hope to keep moving forward with what I love to do.

Seeing my Past in Others

I met a young man in his early twenties who had arrived in Vancouver … leaving his past behind as I did. We met on the streets of the East Side when I was walking around and asked him, "You're too young to be down here, what are you doing on these streets?" Young people didn't last too long down here, everything about them would change for the worse within a few months. He reminded me of myself when I had arrived in Vancouver, down in one of the filthiest, most dangerous alleyways in the East Side … a place where people used drugs, got beat up and robbed.

After asking him what he was doing, I introduced myself, "Hi, my name is Jemal," and told him about UGM. He agreed to go for a coffee to talk about my work, my life, and about hope. He listened as I told him about my past and after a while, he said, "Jemal, after hearing your story, I want to come and do the program."

To me, he was like a young kid searching for a new life. Seeing him over the next while, mentoring and correcting his ways, I began to forget about my past, and I started to sleep well without many nightmares. After he finished the program and I had moved out of my MMP apartment, I gave it to him … along with all my furnishing so that he could move in right away . We spent a lot of time together, taking him to Bible studies, church, and I even baptized him. He was like a close brother to me. It was amazing seeing and hearing him telling his testimony about his past life. I felt and thought, "You know what, God is working, this is why He saved me. God has a plan for my life." I knew it without a doubt.

I felt happier, proud of myself, seeking God's will in everything I did from that moment forward.

This young man's story touched me the most. Like me, he was running from a gang, and I could understand and relate to him. Because I had opened up to him about my past, he trusted me. He went to school in Vancouver and then moved back home. Now he has a wife and kids, he's doing well and keeps in touch with me. It's an incredible story about how God can change a life by His mercy and grace.

I can't help but smile when I think about the people that I have helped getting clean and sober, getting their lives back on track, and their families back. . It's such a blessing to see God's hand in transforming souls from being lost and broken, into someone so different, something that they could not do themselves, only God could do. I am so grateful that God has answered my daily prayers … for His glory.

Chapter 10

Connected With His People

I often think back to my early days at UGM. Countless people helped me to grow spiritually, to become a better person, and have compassion for people less fortunate, it's something that I cherish every day.

Meeting Jack Summerfield soon after I entered the UGM program was a moment I will never forget. I was shy of him at first until he began helping me with my struggles … I could hardly wait to see him the next day. He knew scripture inside and out, a gentle, humble man who helped people learn God's word and feel good about themselves. I told Jack that I was a Muslim and he said, "You're a Muslim? UGM is a Christian program." I replied, "I don't care, it doesn't matter, I need help."

When he asked if he could pray for me, I said, "Sure," because I trusted him, and had a feeling that he was close to God … I wanted all the help available. I don't remember much of what Jack and I talked about, but I do recall the prayers for hours on end. Jack taught and inspired me to pray for people, attend Bible studies and church. It was like God's spirit talking to me through Jack.

Pastor Rene was another person I connected with when he was preaching one day at UGM. When he gave me a Bible, I said, "Rene, I can't read it." He replied, "That's okay, you take it and hold onto it … one day you will read it." When I was in the shelter and couldn't sleep, I often prayed, asking, "God, here I am …do you want me to leave UGM or stay. I need your help." It didn't take long before I was able to read some scriptures, and then pray for myself and other people.

I went to AA meetings at the mission and meetings outside at the Native Friendship Center, Keefer House, the Alano Club, and many other places in Vancouver. These meetings helped me a lot, listening to stories about other people's addictions and how they had broken free. After a while, I spent more time reading the Bible and going to church. Today, I have a more balanced life, spending time with people in the community and helping where needed.

It's such an incredible feeling, to work and serve God and I love my job. That's why I smile so much … it's exciting. Every day, I ask God, "Who am I going to help today?" God's love has changed so many lives, especially mine, and put the best people in my life at His perfect timing. One of my dear Christian friends is Joanne, a prayer warrior with deep empathy that has helped me many times when I was feeling down, confused and struggling.

After I graduated the program in 2006, I went to Joanne and asked her about going into ministry volunteering with Alpha, but there was a strict policy where people needed one year clean and sober before volunteering. It was a policy that Joanne couldn't relax, wave or make exceptions to, not even for me. When she said, "No," I replied with, "okay," and then walked away … a little upset. I felt rejected but I didn't take it personally. She encouraged me to get involved volunteering at my own Broadway Church first before coming into 'the war-zone,' as she and many called it, in the downtown East Side.

Joanne was right, being involved in the ministry at UGM at that early time in my recovery was too much and too soon. I began to connect on a personal level of understanding, trust and respect. I love Joanne … she has a beautiful heart and kind spirit. She doesn't see me as an addict, she sees me as a human being.

After that meeting with Joanne, I went down and spoke to Kumar about my feelings. As always, he's a good listener, and I took his and Joanne's advice about volunteering at Broadway Church. When I look back at it now, I was anxious for nothing.

It wasn't long before the new UGM chaplain offered me a position at UGM's drop-in centre but I turned him down because of some things in my life that I wanted to clean up before moving forward into ministry. I told him,

"I'm not ready yet," and left it at that. Joanne was so happy when she heard that I had turned down the offer.

Joanne continued to watch and pray for me. One cool thing that happened from knowing her is meeting her parents while I was working at the Thrift Store. Her mom and I became close friends, and I would visit her at home. We would stand out on the porch talking about my story and many other things. We became such close friends that I often asked Joanne, "How's your mom?" … and her mom would ask Joanne, "How's Jemal doing?" My precious relationship circle was growing more each day, with not only new, trusted friends, but also their relatives and friends.

Around this time, I began to think about my daughter living in Montreal. She was a teenager, and I often prayed about her, asking God, "I just want to meet her and see her face." I didn't ask God for a long-term relationship, just that I could see her at least once. For eight years, I kept praying, and had faith that one day God would answer my prayers.

I was watching the Super Bowl football game one afternoon with Peter and other friends when my cellphone rang. I looked at the incoming number on my display and saw it was a 514 area code from Montreal. I answered the call and heard, "Hello, this is your daughter?" I was stunned and replied, "Who?" She answered, "I'm your daughter, don't you want to talk to me?" I was so surprised and speechless, the only thing I could say was, "Can I call you back?" A while later I had enough courage to call her back, thinking, "Just breath, don't be so anxious and nervous."

She answered my call and I said, "I'm sorry I hung up on you, I didn't know what to say." After we talked for a few minutes, I asked her again if I could call her back. After a few weeks of talking and texting, she asked me if she could come for a visit to see me. We spent a few days together, talking and laughing about many things.

I told her I was very sorry for leaving her in Montreal, and that it was not her fault; it was mine. I was crying when I said, "Can you forgive me?" She replied, "Dad, I forgive you, that's why I'm here." She told me that she knew me, but I didn't know her. "What do you mean," I asked? She explained that she learned about me from reading the media coverage of my recovery and new life.

Prayer is so powerful. The same day I was asking God about me seeing my daughter, she was talking to her mom about wanting to contact me. When I think about this today ... about my daughter telling me she forgives me, my eyes tear up. God is such an awesome God; I am grateful beyond words.

Joanne and I often met to talk and pray, she told me that it was especially touching when she saw me preaching at the drop-in centre. She spoke to me about the many blessings she received by watching me grow stronger in

Christ. At the time, she was working with UGM interns who travelled here from Germany.

One of the interns became a dear friend, and we would go for dinner with Joanne and other staff. These group gatherings at restaurants, fish hatcheries and other places are what helped me keep connected to the Christian community.

After Joanne debriefed the interns, she told me about the impact that I was having on them. It lifted my spirit and put a happier smile on my face to hear such things. Indeed, it was quite humbling. I still keep in touch with some of the interns and visited one when I went to Germany to see my brother. He showed me around the country and beautiful areas. It was a time of joy being with my dear friend. A while later, he returned to Canada for a visit and he introduced me to his wife.

When it came time for the 'Courage to Come Back' award, Jeremy from UGM's media department, went to Joanne and asked, "Do you know any people that you think we can talk to about this?" Joanne responded with, "I know it needs to be Jemal."

"Courage to Come Back' is about "British Columbians who have shown courage in the face of extraordinary adversity in their lives to then emerge stronger and with a deep understanding and compassion to help others. Each year, Coast Mental Health recognizes "5 individuals who have overcome their struggles in the areas

128

of mental health, addiction, medical, physical rehabilitation and a youth category that encompasses all the others. Through sharing these individuals' stories, we [Coast Mental Health] keep mental health in mainstream conversation and remind everyone that overcoming extraordinary adversity is possible. The Courage to Come Back Awards, we share their stories of triumph with the goal of helping others who face adversity in their own lives, regain the belief that reclaiming their lives as possible. Sharing the recipients' stories also brings awareness to mental health as a common thread through so much of the human condition."

For me, this was a chance to talk about my addiction, how and where it began, and to tell my story to a wider group of people. It certainly does take courage to come back from many years of addiction, and my hope is that by talking about my own journey, it will help others see that it can be done … with God's help.

It was amazing to hear about the award, something that made me a little anxious at the time, but I felt grateful and blessed to have this opportunity to give back to the community and give God the glory for what He did in my life. I was honoured and humbled to receive this award in 2016.

With all of my past experiences and memories of the violence that I had witnessed, I think Joanne hugely helped me about the appropriate way of responding to incidents I was involved in as an outreach worker. She remembers well, the numerous times that I had to deal with … or avoid being in confrontation with people that came to UGM for help or when I was preaching.

My memory of one person grabbing me and chasing me around the drop-in centre makes me laugh now, but it wasn't funny at the time, others were laughing, but not me. I just kept preaching God's word … about forgiveness. Finally, the other outreach staff came and helped the person calm down.

What hurts me profoundly is remembering my close friends who relapsed. Not only does it anger me because I sometimes don't understand why … it brings me to tears when I see and feel their pain. Not just my friends who relapse, but whenever I'm working outreach and talking to people on the streets suffering from addiction … I have to wipe the tears from my eyes. I know and feel the suffering, the pain, fear, and feelings of hopelessness. Like Joanne, one of my spiritual gifts is empathy, and I'm so grateful and blessed to have these feelings. Only through daily prayers and devotions am I able to see His light and love for vulnerable people who are struggling with life.

Throughout my journey, Joanne was on my heart many times when she was in the hospital waiting for surgery. I was praying for her one evening, and God gave me a vision. As she lay on the operating table, I saw Jesus standing beside her with His hand on her. When I woke up, I went and told Kumar and said, "Kumar, I saw a vision of

Jesus standing over Joanne and healing her." Kumar said, 'C'mon, let's go to the hospital and visit her."

She didn't want to have any visitors yet, but when we arrived at the hospital, she was up out of her bed. We went into a room and sat down together, and I told her about my vision. She said that when she went into the operating room for surgery, they had a terrible time getting the IV in her, but she had a sense that someone was holding her hand. She said she realized later that there was nobody there, that it was Jesus keeping her safe and healing her. Joanne is now clear of cancer for over three years.

I began volunteering with Matt, the mission Chaplain, helping make sandwiches to serve to those who were hungry. We were still at the old UGM building then, and I was sorting through the bins of donations. We were involved in moving clothes back and forth and setting up booths.

One especially memorable time with Matt was when a group of UGM Alumni went to Bowen Island, Rivendell Retreat where Matt was the facilitator. It was Matt's first year working in outreach when we began a deeper relationship with each other as co-workers and friends. This Rivendell trip was one of the hardest, physically demanding trips ever. We were trail-blazing and threw chunks of firewood down the hill. I was down at the bottom … ducking and dodging wood as the pieces tumbled towards me.

When we returned from Rivendell, I began working full time on the UGM outreach team … a smooth transition with Matt being my supervisor. We worked shoulder to shoulder on the breadline and at meal times, where we met and connected with many of the East Side population. Matt would play his guitar during praise and worship, and I would share God's word. These are the times when, after me sharing my story, Matt learned more about me and my past.

It was not smiles all the time. I experienced some tough times in the spiritual realm when people who listened to me preach would attack me. Also, there were many people suffering from mental illness, and we would talk and listen to them out by the back gate. It's getting much worse now than previous years.

Today, I see a lot of mental illness all over the streets, and at UGM. It's easy to tell when someone is suffering from this illness, especially when I see and talk to a person a few months or years ago, compared to today. Many are very different people, lonely, depressed, and some suffering from months of psychosis. Even in the short term, like when people finish the six-month UGM program and then relapse. When they come back a few weeks or months later, they are far worse off mentally. I see how using toxic crystal meth has affected their minds.

Street drugs are much dirtier now than they were before; mixed with substances unknown to the addict. Some who are prescribed medication for mental illness fail to take it; instead, they use whatever will help them quickly numb their emotional pain. It's so sad to see. However, when I walk the streets, it's a wake-up call for me when I see and listen to such chaos and torment. I think Jesus is showing me what would happen if I ever relapsed; which, by the grace of God, will never happen.

Before I would go for my walks on the East Side, Matt would insist we pray together.. The devil enjoys using his devices to create spiritual storms and bring down God's disciples.

Ephesians 6:10-18. "Therefore put on the full armour of God, so that when the day of evil comes, you may be able to stand your ground, and after you have done everything, to stand. Stand firm then, with the belt of truth buckled around your waist, with the breastplate of righteousness in place, and with your feet fitted with the readiness that comes from the gospel of peace. In addition to all this, take up the shield of faith, with which you can extinguish all the flaming arrows of the evil one. Take the helmet of salvation and the sword of the Spirit, which is the word of God. And pray in the Spirit on all occasions with all kinds of prayers and requests. With this in mind, be alert and always keep on praying for all the Lord's people."

No matter what happened, I was able to weather the adversity … keeping my eyes on Jesus. At the time, I was still learning to speak English by talking, and I suppose some people had trouble understanding what I was saying. Matt encouraged me to keep on doing what I was doing, supporting me in all I did. When I was struggling with some of my past, he was there to listen, advise and pray. He was more than a supervisor to me. We are brothers in Christ. Matt often jokes, "Jemal, you're a brother from another mother."

I was still only dating Vincia at that time when we would visit Matt over at his tiny basement suite where I had to duck my head because of the low ceiling. Just like with Joanne, I became good friends with Matt's parents. I first met his family at banquets where I told my story, then again Mission's Fest in Vancouver. It's amazing how God puts people in our lives where we can all encourage each other and talk about God's wisdom, peace and glory.

Matt and I married our wives and became fathers around the same time … our children were born only six months apart. At my wedding, Matt played his guitar and did whatever he could to help with the ceremony.

When I was praying about my dream to open a recovery home in Coquitlam, Matt and I talked, prayed about it, and realized that this was not about exiting my ministry at UGM. Matt said, "I would be super happy to continue working together with you helping people with their addictions."

One man, who has helped me the most, is Pastor Darin at the Broadway Church whom I met several years ago. After listening to a DVD I gave him about my story, he said, "What God's done in your life, he wants to do in everyone's life in situations like yours." He asked me what I had done that helped me so much. He often asked me for more details, saying, "I can't be hearing the whole story, tell me more about your life."

I didn't want to talk about my life. I would answer his questions, no problem, but I avoided glorifying it. Until I began writing this book, I preferred people didn't know all the details of my past. Now I realize people need to know.

Although I told Pastor Darin only the details that I thought he needed to know to understand my story, I held back on many of the details and the feelings that surrounded them.

I began volunteering for Broadway Church in their warehouse next door at their street ministry where we served over 9,000 meals a year, a food bank open twice a week and helped people who needed clothes. We also conducted services inside the warehouse where I was one of the speakers. I already knew many of the people because some were living on the streets and some from the area near UGM.

One day, Pastor Darin invited me to speak to his staff at a meeting. He told me about how he was trying to help a man and minister to him when he was begging for food. He wanted to build a relationship with the man not just by giving him food and money, but by talking to him.

He attempted to win him over to Christ, but thought to himself, "Am I doing the right thing?" He approached me and said, "Jemal, what should I do? You live and work with these folks." I simply told him the truth, "You're not helping this man by giving him money." He replied, "Then teach me Jemal," and asked me to teach him and his staff about what to do and say.

I talked to the staff about how to approach and talk to people who were struggling to survive on the streets … what to do, what not to do. There were about fifty people in the room, who listened carefully and peppered me with questions. Sometimes it's difficult for people to understand why it's not a good thing to give food or money to people who are living on the streets and homeless. Providing food in a sealed baggie is the best way to help feed someone who is hungry, but handing them canned food that, more likely than not, may be sold on the streets to buy alcohol or drugs is not the thing to do.

This is why giving money is a no, no. God's word says, "If among you, one of your brothers should become poor, in any of your towns within your land that the Lord your God is giving you, you shall not harden your heart or shut your hand against your poor brother." However, this is not about hardening one's heart; it is about being wise and not enabling.

After my talk, Pastor Darin understood, saying, "Good, now I know and don't feel guilty about not giving money." I felt happy about being able to help, but really, the Pastor was my mentor. I could go to him anytime and talk about anything … if not in person, by phone or text message. For years, he wanted me to join his staff at the Broadway Church, but I was committed to staying in the position I loved at UGM.

My Pastor has always been there for me through good and bad times, especially when I think back to when I was traumatized by seeing my friend die from an overdose. I tried to find and talk to a counsellor at UGM, but nobody was there that day or answered my messages. I felt that if I didn't speak to someone right away after seeing my friend lying dead in the hallway, I might have relapsed. God had someone else in mind for me, and that is something that I will never forget and I still use today. Pastor Darin equipped me with a skill to handle that horrific trauma.

He had me close my eyes, then said, "Trust me here and go back there in your mind to what happened. What do you see? Tell me what is going on. Now, we understand that Christ is present in our lives because He was there at that moment. Ask Jesus to show you where you were standing."

I looked around, and my spirit saw Jesus. Now, for the rest of my life when I picture being back in that traumatic moment, I cannot see it without Jesus being there. I am not alone … Jesus is there with me.

Psalm 23:4 "Even when I walk through the darkest valley, I will not be afraid, for you are close beside me. Your rod and your staff protect and comfort me." Pastor Darin calls this technique "practicing the presence."

He asked my wife and I when I was writing this book, "By writing this book … what if it's a success? Everyone will be sitting across from you and saying, "So tell me, I read in chapter three about this and that, and you're going to be sucked right back there again … are you ready for this?" I replied, "I believe that God has prepared me for this because I've been talking about it for the past four years, and still talking about it today. It's getting easier now, telling people about all the past addictions that God delivered me from."

Chapter 11

A Slave for the Devil until Death to Self

When I arrived at UGM, I was sixty pounds lighter than what I weigh today. My body was skinny, my brain depleted, and deep depression gave way to thoughts of suicide. I had no choice but to accept what the program offered me ... a way out of misery or stay out on the streets of death in Vancouver's East Side. I wanted to live, but not with the continuous turmoil in my mind.

If the devil had his way, death would have arrived soon. I look at it this way: I was the devil's slave. When I was drinking, using drugs and involved in gangs, the evil one loved what I was doing to further his cause of destruction ... his lies kept me doing the things I didn't want to do. Now, after giving my life to Jesus, I was not much value to him. Sure, my life is not perfect, it's not free from fleeting, dark thoughts or occasionally feeling anxiety, but when I turn to God for help, I know that He hears me.

The past trauma I experienced was strenuous to deal with during my time in the UGM rehab program … a process that took many months, even years after. The frightening events haunted me, the memories so painful, but also, I struggled with what was missing in my life. I had a few memories from my childhood before being forced into the war … hugs from my mom, playing and laughing with my friends, but those happy, loving feelings were now gone.

The first few months were depressing. I felt empty, lost, confused and often wondered if I would ever feel normal again. Being surrounded by men who also suffered from trauma and addiction helped somewhat, but nobody could feel the pain deep inside me. I wished I could wake up each morning and flick a switch, turning off all the bad memories. Instead, I had to take baby steps … talking about my pain to people who understood, validated my feelings, and gave me hope, one day at a time.

Some people have asked me, "What did you do, how did you manage to make it through the trauma?" At first, it was quite a challenge because I didn't know what forgiveness was. I didn't know how to forgive those who had harmed me … and I did horrible things in my past. It made me feel sick to think about it. How do you forgive yourself and others who killed your friends, who tortured you and others in prison? I hated what happened … I had deep-seated feelings of anger and hate. For years, I dragged a suitcase filled with pain wherever I went … each place I ran to, it became heavier.

Once my mind began to clear, I often thought about my life. I tried not to think about it, but my mind kept bringing it back, especially at night when trying to sleep.

When we were swimming out to the ship in Ethiopia where my friends drowned, I was angry with the God I knew, Allah. "Why did He allow this to happen … why? What a mean God," I thought. I could not understand the craziness of people dying this way right beside me. I did notice that the two swimmers, who knew they would soon drown, had peace about their demise. They were Christians. At the same time, I questioned God, "What did I do wrong, why have I been here suffering in the water for three days … why, why, why?"

Only when I learned how to read scriptures, pray and seek help … only then did I begin to understand and have some relief and peace in my mind. I knew that when I came to Christ, He gave me freedom, a new life, new hope, and a way to let my troubles go. The most important thing was learning how to forgive.

Not just say in my mind, "I forgive you," … but make a deliberate decision to release feelings of resentment or vengeance towards the soldiers and prison guards who harmed me, regardless of whether they deserve my forgiveness. It wasn't a cure-all action with every negative feeling suddenly gone, but it helped a lot. My pain was a lot less as I grew closer to God. Mark 11:25 says, "And, whenever you stand praying, forgive, if you have anything against anyone, so that your Father also who is in heaven may forgive you your trespasses."

It's not that I have forgotten my dark past, but now I'm able to put these memories aside, thinking about them only occasionally, like when writing this book or sharing my story with someone I want to help. Alcohol used to be my best friend before real friends came into my life, and God is now my best friend above all others. He is my advocate, advisor, redeemer, and my saviour for all time.

I refuse to let the devil tell me that I'm worthless because he's been a liar from the beginning. Success is not something I see in others or when reaching a remarkable goal ... it's because our lives do not reveal marks of failure or depression, helplessness or sickness. Success is something seen in a smile, acts of kindness, compassion and love. It's in one's demeanour which glows serenity, happiness, joy, and peace.

My Steps to Recovery and Healing

Before beginning my journey with God by my side, I had to learn about the steps in Alcoholics Anonymous (AA). UGM uses these Christian-based steps as a foundation in their recovery program. The first step was the longest and most important for me to do, "We admitted we were powerless over alcohol - that our lives had become unmanageable." It was hard for me to admit that I couldn't control my thoughts and my actions.

I believe that I had a life-threatening problem and wanted help letting go of my past. It wasn't easy, but by knowing and admitting powerlessness, it was the beginning of breaking the cycle of my addiction that I was stuck in for most of my life. Alcoholics Anonymous believes that by admitting you can't control your alcohol use is a necessary first step on the path to recovery. I learned that just reading the '12 Steps' literature was not enough; I had to put into action what I was reading … "working the steps."

I didn't know anything about what to do, where to begin or how to do it. Staff and Alumni helped me along saying, "The healing starts here in Step 1, and that I couldn't move forward in my recovery until I got this one right. There isn't a right or wrong way. Every person goes through the program the way that works best for him or her. For me, I believed in my heart what Kumar told me about my addiction. It was not my fault morally … it was a disease. At the time, I didn't care what it was. I wanted help no matter what I had to do or believe … I wanted out. I had to surrender, be humble, honest, and be willing to change.

Romans 7:18: "And I know that nothing good lives in me, that is, in my sinful nature. I want to do what is right, but I can't."

The crucial step for me was realizing that I had hit bottom. Without getting help right now, I knew that I would end up in prison or die on the streets. I was desperate beyond words. At first, I thought my problems stemmed from using drugs and drinking, but I was wrong. When I was high, it was impossible to stop. I was obsessed and powerless every day, in a continuous cycle that led me into dark places of despair, physically, mentally, spiritually, and emotionally.

It wasn't only my drug and alcohol use that nearly killed me. It was all of my addictions that dragged me away from reality, into self-centeredness and blaming others for my problems. I was at a point in my life where I could no longer deny or refuse to believe I had a problem.

How and why was I powerless? Does my personality change when I'm using? How did my addiction hurt or destroy my relationships with others who cared about me? I had to examine, learn and work through all this mess in my life. My outward behaviour began to change, my inner feelings and thoughts calmed down and reversed from being antisocial to social. I knew that if I held back, that I would eventually relapse, I had to stop delaying, and start my journey to recovery one step at a time

My counsellor insisted that I take all the time I needed to think about, and work through the recovery process. Rushing would defeat the purpose of getting it right, risking a relapse and more pain if not dealt with properly. I opened my mind and listened carefully to what people told me. After understanding and knowing without a doubt that I was an addict, I was at peace. I could now move on without feeling shame or guilt.

As I moved on, I realized and began to believe that only a power higher than myself could restore me to sanity.

Even though I understood, I still suffered from pain and depression at times. Thoughts about using again were in my mind when I felt angry, empty or confused. You see, when I was in my addiction, I kept making the same mistakes repeatedly … not realizing the insanity of it all. I had lost faith in Allah a long time ago, putting my belief in a box with a sealed lid. I was still mad at God and wanted nothing to do with Him.

At first, because I didn't trust people or God, I had trouble understanding who or what they meant by "a power greater than ourselves." At the AA meetings, I went to … not many talked about the bible or Jesus. They spoke about how messed up they were when using, how they were doing now, and some shared their hopes for tomorrow. Many members explained what they were doing in their everyday lives, but not much about how they were feeling inside. I sat there and listened for a few weeks before having the courage to go up in front of the crowd to speak.

Slowly, I learned how the AA program was not one of religion it was about spirituality. I knew that I wasn't able to survive on my own; I needed a power that loved me and cared about my life. As my mind cleared, I started thinking about this God, which people often talked about …, and how He had changed their lives. I had tried everything else to numb my pain, "Why not try this new God," I thought.

However, my mind always wanted instant relief from pain, instant answers, everything right now. Although I knew there was a God, I still had memories of not trusting Him, "Why don't you help me … why is this happening to me if you love me?" I didn't have high expectations with UGM at first, but I was willing to try, to believe and have hope. I started to feel loved, and gave my entire life over to Jesus, my personal saviour.

I started to go to church and bible studies. This helped me not only have faith but also practice what I believed. Occasionally, I asked myself, "How could I put complete trust and faith in God after what I had gone through for so long?" I couldn't just push these issues under a rug, or sweep them out the door. That was not going to help, and I knew it. I needed more … I wanted more.

Deciding to turn my will and life over to the care of God, as I understood Him, was scary at first. Slowly, I put more trust in Him, one moment and day at a time, choosing to listen and learn. I began to let go of my own will and give more to God. I prayed often and recited the serenity prayer, "God grant me the serenity to accept the things I cannot change, the courage to change the things I can, and the wisdom to know the difference." Even though He knew what I was thinking, I still talked and prayed, asking for help, for peace, and control over my thoughts and decisions.

Romans 12:1: "And so, dear brothers and sisters, I plead with you to give your bodies to God because of all he has done for you. Let them be a living and holy sacrifice— the kind He will find acceptable. This is truly the way to worship Him."

I doubt I would have survived the program without giving my will and life over to the care of God. It was the beginning of not only trusting God but also trusting people.

My counsellor guided me through "making a searching and fearless moral inventory of my life." After being so dishonest for most of my life, it was time to dig deep without fearing what God or another person would think about what I had done to hurt others. I was still ashamed and felt guilty. Unlike my past life of numbing feelings with drugs and other addictions, I now had to be honest, be fearless about my past moral sins, and face reality. I did some things that I didn't want to think or talk about with anyone.

Lamentations 3:40. "Instead, let us test and examine our ways. Let us turn back to the Lord." God asks us to search what our ways have been in the past, and look at whether they have been right or not. Once we examine our lives and make amends to those we have harmed, the changes, at least for me, lead to a path to freedom and well-being.

I didn't write down most of my inventory about my resentments, fears, behaviour, beliefs, and secrets … I talked about them with my counsellor, Kumar. Examining my feelings was the most difficult to do and thinking back to the horrible events and incidents was painful. Sometimes it felt like I was looking at a painful, infected sore that was not healing, and eating away at my flesh and mind.

At first, I wondered why I had to look at this fear and pain again now that I was clean and sober.

I know now that working through this was the best thing I could have done … a process of talking about my pain with God and someone I trusted. Unwrapping my past one page at a time relieved my pain, cleared my thoughts, and gave me peace about myself. I could love myself and others as God loved me.

I revealed the worst parts of me to another person, a Pastor at one of the nearby churches. All my life, I had kept many secrets that I didn't ever want to bring back up or reveal to anyone. Now, here I was … preparing to tell another human being, things that I hidden for decades.

Before visiting the Pastor, I talked to God, confessing my sins, telling him everything that I was about to tell the Pastor. I wanted to do this outside of UGM with someone I could trust to keep our talks confidential. All I knew for sure was that I needed to do the entire program as honestly as possible and do it all … not leaving anything to haunt me in the future. I prayed for courage and willingness to speak the truth, be humble and not fret about what I was about to do.

When I think about it now, I realize that first I had to admit it to myself, then to God, and only then could I talk to the Pastor. "Confess your sins to each other and pray for each other so that you may be healed. The earnest prayer of a righteous person has great power and produces wonderful results."

I began to see a pattern in my character defects that often kept me in my active addictions, and gave me, "The courage to change the things I can." After my two-hour-long meeting with the Pastor, I left the room smiling, feeling light and free from condemnation, guilt and shame. I couldn't stop smiling for days, a feeling that's hard to explain or imagine. I could now accept who I was at this moment, not feeling trapped back in a time where I was living in sin. I had compassion for myself, but more importantly, I felt more caring towards others … feeling what they were struggling with each day.

Psalm 32, 1-2: "Oh, what joy for those whose disobedience is forgiven, whose sin is put out of sight! Yes, what joy for those whose record the Lord has cleared of guilt, whose lives are lived in complete honesty!"

Living a lie is a miserable way to live. I had known the weight of heavy burden and the painful agony of hiding secrets. God already knew my past. I just had to acknowledge and accept it as being in the past and be willing to move forward with His love and forgiveness.

I was ready to have God remove all my defects of character. After understanding the exact nature of my wrongs that I had done to others, God, and myself, I didn't want them to ever bother or burden me again with fear, anger, confusion and resentments. I learned that this was a life-long process of healing that I had to work at daily, through prayer and thanksgiving. If I wanted to stay clean and sober and enjoy life with my wife, son and friends, this new life of freedom and joy was the most important thing to do in my life. Then everything else would fall into place, as God wanted it to be.

Romans 6:5-11: "Since we have been united with him in his death, we will also be raised to life as he was. We know that our old sinful selves were crucified with Christ so that sin might lose its power in our lives. We are no longer slaves to sin. For when we died with Christ, we were set free from the power of sin. And since we died with Christ, we know we will also live with him. We are sure of this because Christ was raised from the dead, and he will never die again. Death no longer has any power over him. When he died, he died once to break the power of sin. But now that he lives, he lives for the glory of God. So you also should consider yourselves to be dead to the power of sin and alive to God through Christ Jesus."

The only hope I had was to let my old self die and bury my sins in Christ; where I left my defects. As my Life Recovery Bible says, "These character defects can only be removed, never improved." Most of my life I had tried to be a better person, stop using or drinking, but now I know that I can't make a sin better, I have to kill it by confessing and being forgiven.

Instead of dreaming about being a soccer player or movie star as I did when I was young, I now strived for spiritual growth. I began envisioning the person I would like to become ... sharing God's love and helping others who were suffering as I had. I had a hope of reaching my aspirations and dreams of being that person.

Each morning when I woke up, I asked God to remove my defects and shortcomings of impatience, anger, apathy, criticism, judgment or negativity. I know these flaws were not going away by themselves, and I surely can't remove them by myself. When I was on the streets, I swaggered around full of pride and selfishness, not allowing anyone to put me down or intrude into my space. My attitude was changing, and I was living a happier life compared to my past suffering.

1 John 1: "But if we confess our sins to Him, He is faithful and just to forgive us our sins and to cleanse us from all wickedness. If we claim we have not sinned, we are calling God a liar and showing that His word has no place in our hearts."

For me, being humble was the act of confessing and agreeing with God that what His word says to be wrong, is wrong. Once I recognize that I have offended God, I go to Him right away and confess, not wait until tomorrow or the next day . Even if it's the same sin repeatedly, Jesus forgives me. My previous sins washed away forever.

When I am humble before God, the seeds of humility grow. Today I feel a real connection with others, knowing that we all fall prey to the same evils and that we all have dreams for a happier future. It all comes down to my life of daily prayer and not having expectations that God will answer me right away. More often than not, He doesn't, but I leave it in His hands, knowing that He is in control, He had perfect timing and will answer me the time is right.

That is how I learned patience and trust, living a more spiritual life. No matter what life throws my way to discourage me, I am not powerless anymore as I was when in active addiction.

I made a list of all the people that I had harmed and became willing to make amends to them all. Of course, it was painful for me. It was hard to remember some of the people that I had harmed. When I lay down to go to sleep at night, I kept a pen and paper beside me so that when I did remember, I could write it down and not forget again. I had a long, long list that covered several pages.

This process was wearing me down, but my sponsor, pastor, and Kumar helped me through. There are so many ways to harm a person, and I did every one of them. I not only had to write their names down on paper, but also, what happened ... and what I did to them. The process brought back unwanted memories of my past and the times that I preferred not to think about anymore. Then I had to discuss each one of these with my sponsor or some wise person willing to help me.

I made direct amends to people wherever possible, except when to do so would injure them or others. I had to apologize to people I had harmed. My sponsor told me that this would help give me peace of mind and remove my feelings of regret if I was ready and willing to take the full consequences of my past actions. These, coupled with taking responsibility for the well-being of others made me nervous and anxious. If I would do more harm than good by apologizing, it was best not to try.

I didn't realize at the beginning that it may take many years, or that I may never be able to make amends because the person had passed away or some would refuse to hear me. I wrote down a monster-resentment that I had against someone in Oregon. He did something against me that I will never forget. When I phoned to tell him I forgave him, he said he didn't remember. It made me so angry while we were talking and I couldn't believe or understand how he could forget such a mean thing. Shortly after, I let it go and carried on.

With some attempts to make amends, I had to let go of expectations and fears of rejection. It was important for me not to focus on what the outcome would be, and realign my thoughts on why I was doing this.

Mathew 5:23-25: "So if you are presenting a sacrifice at the altar in the Temple and you suddenly remember that someone has something against you; leave your sacrifice there at the altar. Go and be reconciled to that person. Then come and offer your sacrifice to God. When you are on the way to court with your adversary, settle your differences quickly. Otherwise, your accuser may hand you over to the judge, who will hand you over to an officer, and you will be thrown into prison."

Making direct amends by meeting with them or talking on the phone was the most difficult for me to do. Writing a letter was much more comfortable because none of them wrote me back. Going to Ethiopia to make amends was very hard, and I'm grateful it took me about seven years before I did it. I was more grounded and stronger with my faith in God then. This trip ended well as I was able to tell people about how I had changed my life, and shared with them about how God's love had helped me. This essential step helped me to understand the power of humility, love, and forgiveness.

I continued to take my personal inventory and when I was wrong, I promptly admitted it. My spiritual wellbeing is the most important thing for me. Instead of focusing on the negatives that creep in, I look at the good things in life … the good in people as opposed to their faults. Of course, I am frustrated at times, who isn't? This is life, but what I do or how I act when trials come my way, is my choice. I can react with anger or smile and love the person for who they are. When I'm wrong about something, I admit it and change my thinking or actions.

1 Corinthians 10:12-13: "If you think you are standing strong, be careful not to fall. The temptations in your life are no different from what others experience. And God is faithful. He will not allow the temptation to be more than you can stand. When you are tempted, he will show you a way out so that you can endure."

Once I understood and believed this in my mind and heart, my life was much happier … my faith was secure in knowing that I could stand firm and stable without succumbing to temptation.

I sought through prayer and meditation to improve my conscious contact with God, praying only for knowledge of His will for me and the power to carry that out. It was easy for me to do, as I had already given my life over to Christ and was close to Him on a daily basis.

Colossians 4:2: "Devote yourselves to prayer with an alert mind and a thankful heart." Being thankful every day is what keeps me alive spiritually. God is my higher power, and I'm not ashamed to share His love wherever I go. Putting Him first in my life, even before my wife and son, is what keeps me free from falling. With God being the utmost importance, everything else falls into perfection in His timing, not mine.

As a result of doing the program and listening to God, I try to carry His love to alcoholics and to practice God's principles in everything I do. That is what my life is about now, helping others with their addictions.

Galatians 6:1-3: "Dear brothers and sisters, if another believer is overcome by some sin, you who are godly should gently and humbly help that person back onto the right path. And be careful not to fall into the same temptation yourself. Share each other's burdens, and in this way obey the law of Christ. If you think you are too important to help someone, you are only fooling yourself. You are not that important."

Sharing my story with others who still suffer, helps them to understand that they are not worthless or alone, that there is hope, a way out, and a happier life ahead if they want it and are willing to surrender and try. Lost in sin, spiritually dead, and a slave to the devil most of my past life, today I live as a free person in Christ. First, I had to give up my old way of life, which was a self-centered existence, all about me, chained to my sinful thoughts and acts. Today, it's not all about my life anymore. It's about turning my will over to God and trusting in His will for me..

I was powerless back then but not now. Sure, I am powerless over some fleeting thoughts and desires that occasionally pop into my mind, but I control them and choose not to act on them. . I have the ability and power to say no, or more importantly, say yes to God.

Chapter 12

Addiction affects all Family Members and Friends

Every day I see lost souls suffering from addiction as someone's son or daughter, mom, dad, brother or sister. Entire families are torn apart when a loved is abusing drugs or alcohol. Parents fight with each other over how to deal with their son or daughter. When a parent's child is using drugs and receives all the attention, the other sibling may feel neglected and abandoned. Distressed family members often seek comfort to relieve their feelings of rejection, inner turmoil and depression from the chaos that surrounds them.

Sometimes they seek help and advice from a therapist or talk to a compassionate friend, but more often than not, they find instant relief in prescription medication, alcohol or illegal drugs.

When I was drinking in Ethiopia, I hid what was happening as best I could. My mom knew but didn't tell my dad, making it easier for me to continue without much fear of my dad catching me. My siblings also knew and kept it a secret.

Soon after I arrived in Montreal, my drinking caused my wife stress, anger and depression. She was beside herself most days, not knowing what to do or say. She was embarrassed to be around me when friends and relatives visited. Of course, I didn't realize it at the time, but looking back, I can see now how my drinking and behaviour was something that caused my wife much pain and suffering. Once I was clean and sober, just thinking about it filled me with shame and disgust for what I did to her, my daughter, friends and family.

My wife pushed her family away because of my drinking. I probably would have done the same thing if she were a drunk. It hurts to think back to what my daughter had to see and hear. She could hear us arguing, saw me drunk, and felt the missing love-connection between my wife and I. How could a young child not grasp what was happening? It was my fault, and I knew it, but I still couldn't stop drinking.

I felt unworthy to be a husband or father. My daughter saw me when I came home from bars … beaten up from fights, my eyes cut and swollen. Even my party friends were disgusted with my behaviour. They didn't want to be near me anymore. I was at the point where if I had money, I was drinking.

No matter what I did or how my wife tried to help me, nothing changed. It was as if I had cancer and there was no cure. Drink, pass out, drink, pass out, that was the life my wife and child had to live with for years. Running away to Oregon didn't help, it became worse as I drank even more to numb the pain and distance my mind from feelings of shame and guilt.

My life was like a dirty snowball rolling down a hill, hitting everyone in my destructive path. Every person I affected, or perhaps a better word is 'infected' with my disease, they, in turn, affected others with their feelings of anger and disgust. I see it even now if I'm angry my mood changes, and as my mood changes for the worse, people around me see it. Who is happy being around a drunk or someone high on drugs? It's like a domino effect. My actions caused a direct reaction to others.

Living at my Peter's house in Oregon was a nightmare for his wife and child until my friend asked me to leave. When I quit my job and moved in with my girlfriend, she suffered from my crazy, drunken behaviour. When we invited friends over, quiet, fun parties turned into arguments and fights. She tried to help me by having her friend in recovery talk to me about treatment and sobriety, but I didn't want to hear it … I was fine, in control. I didn't want to hear someone tell me that I needed help.

My boss gave me many chances to stop coming into work drunk or hung over, but nothing stopped me. Drinking was my life, that's all I did until I started using powder cocaine and crack. My boss was paying me good money, but I also cost him money before he fired me because I was not working as well as I could if I was sober.

When my wife had had enough and left for Texas, I met a woman who moved in with me. She drank and used drugs, and it was the beginning of my spiral down into using more toxic and deadly substances.

Even the Christian woman I met before I moved to Vancouver suffered from my addictions. Her children saw me drinking in the living room, and she began to smoke pot. She gave me money and I crashed her car. Wherever I lived, I brought disaster to everyone around me.

When I was a gang member, I was addicted to money. The more I had, the more I wanted ... just like booze and crack. The money gave me a high just like a gambler in a casino when he wins. Cash, cards and jewelry were my idols, 'the root of all evil' as they say.

When my best friend Tim in Oregon died from an overdose, it affected his entire family and all his friends. It was my fault for not sending him home. I rented the hotel room where we used drugs together. I didn't insist he leave because I was selfish. If he had left, I would be by myself and lonely. He had a wife, three children and other family and friends who loved him. I didn't dare to visit them ... shame and fear ran wild in my mind.

I blamed myself for Tim's death, not the drugs. All his family members were traumatized, and all of the people connected to them were affected. These were people I sat down and had dinner with them in their homes. Can you imagine being the cause of your friend's death, and the source of his children, brothers, sisters and parent's pain and suffering for years because of something you did so selfishly? Today I can look back at it and see the pain I caused and how many people it affected.

Moving to Vancouver didn't help; I hurt even more people. The drug scene here was wilder and crazier than Oregon. Every person I met when I was using suffered the consequences of knowing and being around me.

You would think I would have learned about not using drugs alone with someone in a hotel room, especially when my friend overdosed and died in Oregon. One evening at the Astoria Hotel on East Hastings, a woman and I were on a three-day bender of using crack … up for three days with not a wink of sleep. I was too high and messed up to notice that she was using heroin and crack … I just heard the screaming in the hallway.

I opened the door, and there she was, dead on the floor. I walked over and checked her pulse, then closed her eyes. What I noticed the most was how much the people looking at her were traumatized … so much so that I ran scared out of the hotel up to the UGM shelter to hide.

As soon as I entered their program, I noticed how much my actions affected other people. When I was drunk or high, I didn't see or understand how much it hurt others. At first, it was seeing how much pain I felt when a close friend in rehab relapsed. I realized that my addiction affected everyone around me the same as I was feeling now about my dead friend. It's not hard to see and feel when you're clean and sober.

I learned even more about it when I was sitting in AA meetings, listening to how others actions, similar to my own had caused so much damage to the people closest to them. I didn't dare to share yet about my life, but as I listened, I cried. The experiences they were talking about were exactly like mine. The meetings brought back painful memories as if it happened that day. For two weeks, I just sat and listened with saying a word about my life as an addict. I had so much guilt and shame that I told myself I didn't deserve to live. I asked myself, "God is going to forgive me? ... no way."

I look at active addiction as leprosy that affects all people who meet the infected person. It spreads like wildfire on the body and inside the mind, which explains why many people call addiction a disease. We can't stop the spread until we stop dragging in the cause. And, if we invite sickness back into our lives, the destruction is much worse. It's as if we took a double dose of what caused our suffering in our previous round of destruction.

Since being at UGM as a resident in the program, and as an employee, I have met some dear, trusted friends-for-life that have similar stories to mine. We hang out, go for coffee and share what's in our hearts. What we have gone through and how we survived, is a journey that many have suffered through, something most people could not imagine. Words are not enough compared to feelings. My friend Alex, whom I had met in 2008, told me his story of traumatic abuse and his inner turmoil that had lasted for decades.

Alex was reluctant to enter the UGM program because it was Christian-based. He is a 'Residential School' survivor, which was, at the time, compulsory for First Nations children. The system harmed Indigenous children significantly by removing them from their families, depriving them of their ancestral languages, exposing many of them to physical and sexual abuse. These residential schools, operated by Catholic and Protestant churches, were horrific, and Alex lived with resentment and hate for decades after leaving.

To numb his traumatic pain due to sexual abuse, he succumbed to drugs and alcohol, a combined and painful experience that he carried with him for much of his life.

Alex and I shared our sympathy, compassion and tears with each other as we shared our stories, but it was a few years before we could share our entire story … reliving old traumas is painful. Alex told me about the sexual abuse, why he drank, and why he was afraid of being at UGM.

He feared to be under another Christian authority as he was in the Residential Schools who wielded power and abuse over him as a child, saying, "If you don't obey, God is going to punish you." Alex grew up hating religion and had no trust for anyone in authority. His story reminded me of when I was back in the Ethiopian civil war when I was psychologically and physically abused and tortured by prison guards.

Alex's parents died when he was eight years old, as an orphan he was raised in various foster homes. He saw alcohol every day, arguing and fights, no love, no close family connections or family values. When listening to his story, my mind reflected back to my past, filled with turmoil for so many years. As teenagers, we both ran away from our unhappy lives, numbing our pain with alcohol and drugs.

After living in a home where a married couple drank a case of whisky weekly, forcing Alex to work long hours without pay, he jumped out a window and ran away. While crossing a highway over to a truck stop, police pulled up and arrested him for something he hadn't done. At the station, he was interrogated for hours, not allowed to use the washroom or make a phone call. The police locked him up until the judge released him on his own recognizance.

It was cold, snowing, and he had no place to stay. Many of the abusive memories returned, and he began drinking to keep warm, and to block out the cold. Alex thought that he had found the solution, the same as I had for decades. Although he had brief times of abstinence, his addiction to alcohol slowly progressed, losing control.

On several occasions, Alex thought about and had many failed suicide attempts. Today, he tells me that, "I believe that God was protecting me all these years."

He was in and out of homelessness, had a bad experience being in a drug rehab centre in the Fraser Valley, only seeing a counsellor once in three months. Finally, after many relapses, he arrived at UGM when he was 47 years old. Unlike me, Alex didn't live on the streets of Vancouver … he came directly from Mission, B.C., to treatment at UGM. I met him soon after he arrived and we became close friends.

It took Alex about three years to begin talking to Kumar, and then me about the sexual abuse he had endured as a child. We understood each other about how we felt and why we used drugs and alcohol to kill our pain. He told me how he got through it when he was young, saying, "When the abuses were happening, I learned that if I stopped screaming, it wouldn't last as long. I would put my mind in a safe place, somewhere far away from where I was."

After graduating the UGM program and working in Outreach, Alex told me, "My life has blossomed, so full of light. I'm smiling, happy … and even if I'm having a bad day, I'm happy because I'm waking up sober."

With my wife Vincia, my friends, and God in my life, I'm never lonely. My mind is focused today on positive things as opposed to my dark past. Some days I reflect back to my previous life when someone shares with me about his or her present or past suffering, but now it's easy not to feel the pain as I used to. Perhaps God allowed me to go through my past so I can understand today what people are feeling and why they are drug addicts or alcoholics.

I know the feeling and what it's like to walk the broken and difficult road. I see people in the line-up at UGM. They are hungry, cold and tired. I can relate to them because I have been in their shoes. I give and help the best I can as if someone was helping me.

Today, many people ask me, "Why is my son or daughter, dad or mom using drugs?" In most cases, it's pain and past trauma, that for the addicts, the only solution they know is using alcohol or drugs or both to numb that pain. Another one of my friend's, like Alex's story, and many others, reminds me of my past pain of terror and death.

Gerry, (not his real name), shared his story and feelings with me, a story that may help others understand why people need to self-medicate.

He started drinking with his gang of friends at age thirteen. He felt included and accepted by friends at drinking parties, where it was normal to join in. They were allowed to drink at home, so Gerry drank with them. He told me, "My parents started seeing a change in me and smelled booze on me when I came home, asking me what I was doing." Unlike many homes that are chaotic and abusive, he had loving foster parents who cared for him and treated him like a son. However, the need to use drugs or alcohol to numb pain can happen fast when a horrific event knocks on the door ..., which was the case for Gerry.

'Grounding' didn't help him stop drinking; he climbed out his bedroom window and snuck out. It was fun to drink and hang out with his friends until the police knocked on the door when he was sixteen years old.

He opened the door and listened as the officer told him his parents were dead from being stabbed and shot to death. Gerry explained to me that, "This is when and why I lost hope in everything. From that time on, I just wanted to numb-out so I couldn't feel the pain." He wondered the same thing as I did, "God where are you, where's this, where's that?"

After living in Toronto for ten years, he ran to Vancouver, carrying all his pain with him. Gerry's story was similar to mine, living on the streets, sleeping under bridges, and thoughts of suicide. His boss fired him, his marriage was at an end, and he lost everything. It was cold and wet outside when he stood on a bridge with a cement brick in his hands. He had planned it so that there would be no possibility of surviving the jump to his death, but something made him change his mind.

It wasn't hard for Gerry to decide to enter the UGM program, he wanted to give life one more chance, "My last chance, if it doesn't work, it's never going to," he said. He read his bible and listened to people in recovery, and began to have hope. Today, Gerry is on a spiritual journey, living a life with God, a life filled with smiles and freedom.

Over the past several years working with people that tell me the same stories of horrific pain, abuse and death, God has given me tears of empathy and compassion. I know how they feel, their fears, hopelessness, and of being slaves to addictions.

As I have grown in God's grace and wisdom, I know now that addiction is like a curse. Sure, it's a disease, but one can recover. Without a doubt, for me, it's about putting God first in my life. Unless I listen to God's Holy Spirit and have a spiritual awakening to what's going on at any one moment, I risk losing my family, my faith, my hope, and my life. The consequences of falling back into my old ways are right in front of me, staring me in the face every time I look at someone suffering from the dregs of addiction.

Chapter 13

Help For Suffering Souls

The Downtown East Side (DTES) is and has been for many decades, a place that engulfs much trauma, suffering and death. Just as when I arrived here, first-time visitors are shocked by what they hear and see. The area is notorious for its level of drug use, poverty, mental illness, homelessness, and other vices.

Not all are born and raised in the DTES ... some arrive here from wealthy families and lost careers. Some have suffered from injuries and sickness while living in a high-end neighbourhood. Years of using and abusing physician prescribed medication, and then being cut-off, they find themselves seeking relief in street drugs. There is so much more to this misery than most people see or even care to know.

However, with many dark stories, there is another side that few people from outside the area see or recognize. Many of the DTES residents take pride in their neighbourhood and say it's not all bad. Their friends and neighbours accept each other as they are, having empathy and compassion for each other. This community is unique compared to other places in Canada. Tent cities pop up overnight on sidewalks, parks, city parking lots, and under bridges.

People living here are lonely, depressed, and often suicidal from trying to cope with the daily struggle of living on these dark streets. But to them, this is their community, their home. They accept each other for who they are. There is no judgment, and they look out for each other when there is violence or police are nearby, protecting each other. People don't call each other "crack-head" or whatever; only the outsiders do. When I lived there, street-people would bring food to me when I was in my tent, just as a friend would do..

Residents have places to meet with friends, get support, access social services, food and shelter. Behind the scenes of addiction and mental illness, there are many intelligent and gifted people. There's a high concentration of incredible artists, including musicians, wood carvers, painters, jewellery makers, and many other talents. I love looking at their creations, hearing the songs, and listening to their stories. It gives me the opportunity to share my past and offer help to those who want it.

DTES Overview

In the 1980s, the area began a rapid decline due to several factors including an influx of hard drugs, the de-institutionalization of mentally ill individuals, policies that pushed prostitution and drug-related activity out of nearby areas, and the cessation of federal funding for social housing.

By 1997, an epidemic of HIV infection and drug overdoses in the DTES led to the declaration of a public health emergency. As of 2017, critical issues are an epidemic of opioid overdoses, especially those involving the drug fentanyl; decrepit and squalid housing and a shortage of low-cost rental housing; and a high prevalence of severe mental illness, which often co-occurs with addiction.

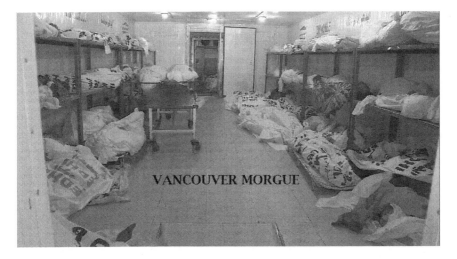
VANCOUVER MORGUE

Numerous efforts have been made to improve the DTES, at an estimated cost of over $1.4 billion as of 2009. Services in the greater DTES area are estimated to cost $360 million per year. Commentators from across the political spectrum have said that little progress has been made in resolving the issues of the neighbourhood as a whole, although there are individual success stories.

Proposals for addressing the issues of the area include increasing investment in social housing, increasing capacity for treating people with addictions and mental illness, making services more distributed across the city and region instead of concentrated in the DTES, and improving coordination of services. However, little agreement exists between the municipal, provincial, and federal governments regarding long-term plans for the area.

What Has and Has Not Worked

With many years of experience during my drug addiction days, and then helping thousands of people during my recovery years, my eyes are now open. They say, "To see it, is to believe it," at least in the physical realm, and I have seen most of it, day in and day out. Each day, month and year, the DTES community degrades further into hell-like scenes of ambulances chasing death.

I stumbled around the DTES for quite some time during my addiction, and often walk into this area today as a Pastor and UGM outreach worker. It's painful to see the suffering souls, shuffling around, faces filled with anguish and torment. Only when one witnesses the images of chaos and death on these streets, can one fathom the depths when words fall short.

More so, the feelings of hopelessness far outweigh what I see every day when looking into their eyes and the sadness that I see there … begging to survive in dark shadows of rejection and fear. Many lay unconscious on the sidewalks or curled up against dirty, storefront walls, pushing a needle in their arms filled with toxic waste. Countless people are in a state of living-suicide that claws away their hope and faith into physical, emotional, and spiritual ruin.

I used to ask, "God, why is it such a mess down here … why are so many people, young and old, suffering from this deadly plague? Why is it so crazy here?" People trapped on the East Side are not only addicted to drugs or alcohol, but many also suffer from mental illness. Some are 'dual diagnosed' with both addiction and mental illness. But why is this Vancouver community notoriously known for such devastation and chaos on every street? Anyone who walks or visits can easily see people tormented by disorders other than addiction.

Senator Larry Campbell, former mayor of Vancouver, boldly reveals why: "When we deinstitutionalized, we promised [mentally ill] people that we would put them into the community and give them the support they needed. But we lied. I think it's one of the worst things we ever did." Many of these people migrated to the DTES community. And there is more to this nightmare, much more.

The Vancouver community social workers are overwhelmed with what they have to deal with every day. I see and talk to people with problems stemming from mental illness, addiction, and sexual abuse. Often, the trauma experienced from sexual abuse leads to alcoholism and addiction. Many patients who were at BC's mental institutions that are now closed, namely, Riverview Hospital, and especially Woodlands Institution, exited after sexually abused and some raped. Many of these 1,700 former residents of Woodlands are still living, many in the DTES. What these patients experienced was horrific.

The provincial government ... confirmed what former residents and their families have been saying for years. Sexual and physical abuses, including beatings, cold showers, burn-inducing hot baths, extended isolation and sexual assaults were rampant at the institution."

Also, I talk to people who were once rational but now suffer from mental illness issues because of chronic abuse of Crack Cocaine and Crystal Meth. These poisons are all over the streets, causing untold misery. So here we have it, as sad as it is. Alcoholism, addiction and mental illness, all mixed in a toxic barrel of suffering.

Living in Hellish Conditions

On March 31, 2017, the BC Non-Profit Housing Association identified 3,605 people in the Metro Vancouver region as being homeless. Of those 1,032 were unsheltered and 2,573 sheltered, the homeless living on the streets, in tents or the bush sleeping under tarps. I visit the homeless using the UGM Mobile outreach van ... bring them food and other necessities. Most people welcome my visit, others shy away, paranoid or afraid of the unknown.

My heart hurts when I see them all alone, living out in the cold and rain. Here is the hidden population, preferring to survive without government help or allowing them to dictate what they must or must not do. My mission is to show them that someone cares about them, and wants to help them if they're willing to accept it.. I don't give them money, instead, a smile, and a lending ear that listens to them, letting them know that someone cares.

Even if the homeless wanted to live in a self-contained room or apartment, there isn't enough available to rent. The vacancy rate is near zero. Many that do move off the streets into social housing find themselves living among mice and rats, bed bugs infecting their skin. Smells of urine, fights, and sirens blasting down the streets are the norm.

Black mould permeates the walls, ceilings, and in many buildings the sinks and toilets in disrepair or plugged. Many of the Single Room Occupancy (SRO) buildings are a disgusting mess with numerous health and safety hazards. Red sores from itchy bug bites cover exposed skin, resembling measles or other contagious outbreaks.

I walk by many of these disgusting buildings, talking to the residents, listening to their horrific stories. It's sad that one of the wealthiest Provinces in Canada allows this to happen year after year.

One of the most notorious buildings in the DTES to warehouse addicts and the homeless is the Balmoral Hotel near Hastings and Main Street, the epicentre of degradation. In July 2018, the city forced the Balmoral to close, citing 60 charges against the owners of the hotel, alleging bylaw violations ranging from rotting walls and floors to faulty plumbing. There are many other hotels in Vancouver offered to the homeless that are little more than rat and bug-infested slums.

What Can Be Done

Having lived in, and seeing the deplorable conditions in the DTES area, as an addict, then as an outreach worker, I know the many problems that face the area. Some say, "Treat the addiction first, then find them housing," others see it the other way around, "Find them home first." What I see is if we find them a place to live before treating their addiction, it often doesn't work. When alcoholics or addicts move in, the tiny homes face damage or destruction from fights, uncleanliness, disrepair, and drug paraphernalia littering the rooms and hallways. I used to live in these rooms … I know what it's like when the rooms fill with partying drug users and dealers every day and night.

For me, I believe that we must treat the addiction first … help them recover mentally and physically, and hopefully, have a spiritual awakening. Without treating addiction first, most people will be back out on the streets, homeless again. Also, we have many people with mental illness issues who need help to maintain their residency, whilst also suffering from substance abuse. Until we treat this group of people, housing in Vancouver will not help them. The ongoing mess is evidence that the system as it is now, is not working.

There are so many programs and charities that help people find a home, offer shelters, meals and clothes, but not near enough detox and treatment facilities. There are waiting lists for both, sometimes two to three weeks before an addict receives help. More often than not, when the date arrives for an addict to go into Vancouver Detox or other places, the drug user has changed their mind or died from an overdose.

When some addicts run out of money, stumbling around sick from withdrawals; the government supplies methadone, Dilaudid, and even prescribe heroin. Although these substances help prevent overdose deaths caused by using fentanyl, the addict remains addicted, chained to a pharmacy and daily visits to the doctor. It's frustrating for me to see all of this happening, and not being able to do enough to change it.

People living on the streets have already lived through years or decades of degradation due to the conditions of their chaotic environment, which surrounds them on every street corner. Addiction and poverty go hand in hand, violating and dragging their dignity into a void of despair. Many live in fear of physical assault, robbery or dying alone. To ease this dread, they press on through each day with mind-altering drugs, not wanting to feel what they regard as an incurable demise. Their minds are empty of hope and ambition.

Many have tried on their own to rid themselves of their addictions, only to ride on a merry-go-round of relapse after relapse, each time falling further into the dark abyss. Often, addicts who used to struggle only with addiction, now suffer from mental illness because of using street drugs. Cocaine, Meth and other intoxicants, mimic bipolar disorder, schizophrenic, psychotic states. Chronic users become paranoid, delusional, fatigued and depressed, exhibiting bizarre behaviours. What property owner, outside the DTES area, would rent their apartment, single room or basement suite to people in active addiction, or dually diagnosed with mental illness?

The Vancouver East Side is like a small town, covering 10-50 square blocks with a dense area of over eight blocks of hell on earth. I don't know any other such place … like a giant warehouse of lost souls crying out for help through tear-stained faces. My heart cries every time I visit and talk to them, feeling their pain. How can we just put them in a room, house them, and not be concerned about their addiction? There are plenty of addiction doctors that prescribe medications, helping patients with their depression, sleepless nights, and physical pain. However, with only treating symptoms, in many cases, their trauma lies dormant, like a sleeping ghost that awakens into a monster of drug addiction.

One of the first classes in the UGM drug treatment program called the 'Dandelion' is the beginning of the road to healing. It's role is to educate on the causes of addiction, and to reveal our hidden trauma and secrets we'd rather not acknowledge.. The outreach worker explains that the dandelion flower has a pretty, outward appearance, but is hard to kill. For most people, this weed is hard to wipe out, always growing again when pulled out, cut off with a lawnmower or whatever.

The root of this menace keeps pushing up new weeds through the ground of life, no matter how many times we think it's gone. With addiction, unless we search for and dig out the root, our enslavement keeps bleeding through our skin. More often than not, those who don't look at the cause of their addiction enter a revolving door of defeat. The relapse rate following a drug rehab program is staggering, often between 50-90% of those who complete the program end up using again.

For me, I kept thinking about using while in the program and for months, after I graduated … right up until I dared to talk to people about my secrets and then I received God's healing. If I had left UGM and obtained housing on the East Side, I wouldn't have lasted one day without using drugs again. It's near impossible to be around all the drug use in such a toxic environment and not use drugs unless you have a healthy, spiritual, support system, and have dealt with the menacing 'Dandelions' in your life.

Perhaps a small percentage can go it alone, but are they living a happy, fulfilled life or are they a 'dry-drunk' … one who no longer drinks or abuses drugs, but continues to behave in dysfunctional ways?

The government is building hundreds of new SRO social housing units to house the homeless and addicts. Steel, portable shipping containers 'are temporary' say city officials, a homeless person or couple can end up living in these units for a year or two while waiting for permanent housing. They look charming, stacked up, resembling tiny apartment complexes.

Each suite measuring 250 square feet has a bathroom and kitchen, steel walls covered and painted, and hardwood floors. One of the new complexes is near where I used to live in a tent, under a bridge. I suppose I would have moved in if it had been offered to me, but I would still be using drugs and messed up in my mind. Who knows if this would have worked for me in the long term? I doubt it. These small modular, self-contained homes, intended for people on welfare, and renters who cannot afford market rates, seldom offer hope of any long-term solution. It does beat sleeping on friend's couch or living alone in a tent, or does it?

When addicted to drugs, living alone in a home can be dangerous and deadly. In 2017, more than 1,200 people died from drug overdoses in the greater Vancouver area. Most people are dying in parks or other isolated locations, with 70% of overdose deaths occurring in private homes, not on the streets.

When someone is sick from heroin addiction, often laced with deadly fentanyl, they use at home; they are too ill to walk to a safe injection site. In the East Side community, hundreds of volunteers and other caring people walk the area carrying Naloxone, a life-saving drug that reverses the effects of opioid overdose. The addict who overdoses while using alone at home usually dies, with nobody there to help and call an ambulance. The overdose crisis in Vancouver is beyond imagination, with emergency departments at Vancouver hospitals treating nearly 5,000 overdoses a year.

The hospital emergency rooms are like a scene from a horror movie. Overdosed addicts sitting on chairs and in beds, nurses injecting more Naloxone every few minutes to keep them alive until a doctor is free to examine them. "We were busy before, now it's just insane," says paramedic Jason Neault. Many of the patients are so severely addicted, their mind confused and dull, that the same patient returns multiple times the same day, overdosed.

Rarely do I walk the East Side community and not see someone near death, lying on the sidewalk with paramedics loading them into an ambulance. Above all other noises in this community are not from cars, trucks and construction, it's from screaming ambulance sirens around the clock. Even though the BC government has declared this crisis a health emergency, it seems a hopeless situation with no immediate solution.

When I walk these streets and visit the homeless, I am overwhelmed at times, wondering, "What can be done … what can I do to help my fellow man?" Sometimes I shake my head, look around, look up and say, "God, please lead me, show me who I can help today." Union Gospel Mission has helped thousands recover from living with addiction, posting this on websites and in the Mission, "Demonstrating the love of Christ; Union Gospel Mission is determined to transform communities by overcoming poverty, homelessness, and addiction … one life at a time."

While government, social services, and health agencies strive to help those most in need, there's only one thing I can do. I do everything I can, helping one person at a time, but I am only one person in a sea of hundreds who need help and support.. I pray that all receive the same gift as I did, a spiritual awakening, faith in God, and passion for helping others in need.

Chapter 14

Married Life – Not Perfect But Centered In Christ

The first time I met my wife-to-be Vincia at the Broadway church in September 2006, it felt like I was living in a fairytale wondering what was going to happen next. It's not a story about love at first sight, but it was the beginning of looking over at a woman that I hoped God wanted in my life. The butterfly feelings made me nervous, an unexpected excitement that had my mind swimming with thoughts about love.

There were about five tables at a small group Bible study called, 'Life Worth Living', with six or eight people at each, and Vincia was sitting across from me. I was scared looking over at her, but it was near impossible for me not to at least glance over to her when she was not looking.

I thought, "Look at her. Could this be the right one? I need your help here God." We didn't speak to each other that day, just listened to others reading some of the course materials. There was a sign-in sheet where I saw Vincia's name and phone number, and of course, I wanted to write it down but felt it wasn't right and decided not to.

Vincia had just started going to the Broadway Church, she had been invited by a friend, and was quite shy. She had just got out of a turbulent relationship that hadn't ended well and wasn't looking for another one. I was confused about Vincia not attending church or courses on a regular basis … she was there, then not. By the end of the course, she saw me out in the hallway, standing near the door talking to someone. I kept glancing over at her until one day I got up the courage to walk over to where she was sitting, eating a meal.

Vincia told me later what she was thinking, "What is wrong with this guy, he's so nervous. Maybe he likes me or something?" She brushed me off that day, but I thought about her day and night, thinking, "I like this woman, God please give me a sign to let me know if my feelings are right or wrong."

We were, and still are, two very different people from opposite backgrounds and lifestyles. When I arrived back at UGM, I asked Kumar what he thought about my feelings. I had made so many mistakes in my past life and hoped that my next relationship, God willing, would be blessed and fruitful. Thinking about Vincia, and how our personalities were so different, like night and day; I couldn't get past thoughts that it would be almost impossible for them to exist together. My hopes of a relationship weren't going to work without me letting go of my will, my desires, and inviting God to direct my path. Vincia was the kind of woman I wanted as my wife, but I wondered if her feelings were the same as mine. My concern was, could she accept me for who I am today, and not judge me for my past?

Kumar told me, "You don't need to have a woman in your life, your needs and desires become like an addiction. Put God first and He will make it work." After we prayed together, I realized that I wasn't the same person I used to be ... I am a child of God, and He wants the best for His children.

During the first six months of visiting and talking to Vincia, I was angry because she wouldn't return my phone calls ... she was working long, twelve hour shifts as a nurse, night and day. I wondered, "What's going on ... why doesn't she contact me, doesn't Vincia like or care about me?" When we did spend time together, we enjoyed going for walks, having coffee and talking. I learned a lot during that time of friendship, what Vincia liked to do, and what she did with the little free time that she had.

I put on my best smile, trying my best to be quiet and patient and listening to what Vincia was saying to me about her life, wants and needs. However, this wasn't the real me, I suppose, not my usual outgoing personality. Being on my best behaviour, I opened doors for her and made sure I was the gentleman I thought she wanted me to be.

When Vincia visited Vancouver's East Side with me, she was shocked. She had never even driven past the area. She discovered there was an entirely different world that she couldn't imagine. When I told her I was addicted to drugs, she didn't believe me. She would laugh, saying, "Ya whatever, you're kidding me, right?"

Even though she learned about my scary past, Vincia didn't see me as a drug addict. When we were at our friend's wedding, and then after driving her home, she thought I was going to kiss her on the lips, but instead, I kissed her on the forehead. For quite some time, I only kissed her on the forehead, something Vincia saw that as strange, wondering, "What was this all about?" After a few months of seeing each other as friends, and then dating, I finally kissed her on the lips. That was when Vincia saw me as a very changed person. She saw me as respectful, and that I wanted to obey God in how we should date.

When I picked her up for dates, my big, gas-guzzling Ford Lincoln stood out like a sore thumb. Not wanting to rush or impose on her privacy, I never went into her home for several months, just phoned to let her know I was waiting outside in my car. The first time I drove her car … I thought she was going to kill me … at least it felt like that.

I parked her car, went upstairs, and waited for Vincia to get ready to go out on date with me. When we went outside, the car was gone. I saw a look on her face that I will never forget. For most people, getting their car towed would not have been such a big deal, but for Vincia, it was huge. She had driven and parked her car for many years and never been towed away for parking in the wrong zone.

Vincia told me that she had lived in a glass house for so many years, not a perfect life, but that she looked at her car being towed away like a stain on her. She had never got a ticket for anything, but here, I drive it the first time, and it disappeared from the roadside.

This unfortunate event had an unexpected consequence in that it helped us to look outside of our world, to see how other people live and react. Sometimes when you're living by yourself, you can be so focused on your own little world that we miss the big picture in a relationship. We need to come into each other's space, learn about each other, and see the positives, not dwelling on imperfections.

After we were married, Vincia was driving her sister to the airport and ran a red light. When she arrived home, she told me, "Jemal, I think a ticket is coming in the mail, I ran a red light this morning." I looked at her and smiled, "Oh', the tables have turned … now you have a ticket just like I did from parking in the wrong place." Life can be so funny at times, smiling and laughing at, and with each other.

Acceptance – Likes and Dislikes

My favourite times for relaxing and enjoying life outside of work are spending time with my wife and son.

Adam loves going fishing and camping, something that Vincia detests and hates to do. We like going to movies together, and Vincia loves to sit by herself, reading a book while eating popcorn. She tried going camping twice with me, it was not something she would ever do again.

For Vincia, she views camping as paying money to be homeless. I laughed when she said, "I pay to live in a home, why would I want to spend time outside and pay." The first time we ventured out into a wilderness park, we stayed inside a cozy cabin, a luxury for most people, but for Vincia, this trip was outside her realm of expectations. She hadn't prepared or packed for the chilly evening and other conditions in the cabin. She was so upset about everything that people thought we were going to break up.

The next trip was real camping, not in a cabin, out on the ground in a tent. Vincia was in the worst mood I've ever seen her. She couldn't believe or accept that sleeping on a blow-up mattress could be fun for anyone. She was far beyond her comfort zone. No regular shower, just a bag of cold water hanging from a tree, no sink, stinky outhouse, and a sore back.

She told me she was thinking, "Some wild animal is going to attack us in this small tent ... what is to prevent them from doing so?" She went on the trip for me after I asked her to go, and if there's one thing I learned for sure, it's to never coax or plead with her into doing something I know she doesn't like.

She was worried all day and night and didn't go fishing, or for walks, friends are telling me that, "Your wife is not happy, she's uncomfortable and mad." She kept saying to me, "Take me home, take me home."

Vincia grew up in the Caribbean where nobody goes camping. Her dad went fishing, without her, but he never did the whole camping thing. "Who would want to leave the warm, sunny beaches and be homeless out in the bush," she said to me. So my camping adventures with my wife again was out of the question, not something we even talk about now, except to laugh about the two times when she did go.

Through all our differences about camping, fishing and swimming, things that Vincia resists doing, she still goes with me and sits in the car reading or whatever. If being out in the dirt-covered forest wasn't bad enough, when we arrived in Ethiopia, I thought she was going to die. She was NOT happy.

We laugh about it now, but it was not funny at the time. We decided to go on a safari adventure trip, out in the hot, humid, unforgiving climate of Africa. Back in the hotel, the electricity had a mind of its own, off one minute, and on the next. Hardly any water in the shower, and when there was, it was cold. We were supposed to stay with my Auntie, but after Vincia experienced the horror in the small village, we went and stayed in a hotel.

Growing up in the Caribbean, Vincia knew what an outhouse was, but at my Aunties, it was very different. Each family didn't have their own; this one was a ghastly, communal affair. She had never heard of such a thing or been around anything like it. When we arrived, it was dark, and she had to use the washroom. My cousin took her along this dark path, and she is thinking, "Where are we going, where is this outhouse?"

She nearly fainted when she opened the door and saw the hole in the ground. It was dark, stinky, nothing to sit on, just a small hole in the dirt that she had to aim for, using a small flashlight. It's hard to imagine what it was like inside this outhouse for Vincia. When she returned, she told me, "The smell was beyond awful. People missed the tiny hole, and the stinky stuff was all over the ground. I felt the blood draining from my face, feeling dizzy and gagging, trying not to throw up." One night was enough and never again. Next, we had to find a hotel. Sounds easy, right?

It was late, and we walked for hours from one hotel to the next in the dark. Because we were foreigners, I told Vincia not to speak any English when we're asking for a room because they would charge us double if they knew. When we found one that had a room available, I talked to the person in charge in my native language. Then Vincia asked, "Do you have a shower?" The man said, "What, she speaks English, she's not Ethiopian." Then he told us the price was higher, and I said, "No, we're going to go find another place." We were so tired that I finally left Vincia in the car while I rented a room. I learned very quickly what she didn't like, and what she couldn't accept.

But it wasn't all bad, visiting Ethiopia opened her eyes to how the people lived without having much, as opposed to how we take things for granted here in Canada. She saw that my Aunt's home was clean every day, removing the rugs, and sweeping the floor. She was in her 70's and a happy person, smiling and grateful for the life she lived as a Christian. Seeing my aunt so content, helped Vincia feel much better about where she was and how blessed of a life we live as a couple.

In The Beginning

Our first year of marriage was a time of getting to know each other, adapting and feeling our way, learning what works and the best paths to take with each other. Before being married, we could go out with our friends without asking or telling each other. Now, it's so much different, in a marvellous way with some very humorous, fun times.

"What are you doing here," my wife asked me one evening. Surprised, I said, "I live here now." "Oh', right," she replied with a smile. I couldn't believe she asked me this question just after we returned home from our honeymoon. With me coming and going for many months at her apartment, it was a big adjustment, realizing and accepting our living together was not a part-time arrangement, it was permanent, a lifelong commitment. We have a lot of laughs and fun today when we talk about our first year together.

Vincia was so used to living by herself that her mind was still in 'single-mode' at times. It took about six months before she talked to others and referred to me as her husband. It was an adjustment period for Vincia, changing her name to Damtawe and such. It wasn't that she didn't want to do it, but it even seemed strange to her when she wrote her new name at work.

It didn't take me long to understand why she wanted a husband that would cook for her. One day, while we were dating, she said she would prepare chicken for dinner. When I arrived home, there it was, all cooked and ready to eat. However, no, she didn't cook the skinny chicken, it was one of those pre-cooked chickens in a plastic case, picked up from the grocery store.

We both like to eat similar foods, except that Vincia and Adam love to eat fried bacon, and I hate the smell of it, and never eat it. She waits until we go out to eat, then smiles with bacon on her plate or in a burger. It was more than eight years before we cooked bacon in our home, and our son Adam loves it.

Even with these minor likes and dislikes, it wasn't as difficult as we sometimes saw with other couples. We jelled, and respected each other for who we were and are today. Of course, there are moments when we don't agree with each other about what we think or do, and we're not much different from other couples.

One Sunday morning when we were getting ready for church, Vincia walked out wearing a pair of dressy, knee-high shorts. They looked nice, but I said, "No, go back and change, you don't go to church dressed like that." She looked at me, not angry, and changed into something more appropriate. In my view, Vincia didn't look at it as me telling her what to wear; she looked at me as caring about her life as it should be in the eyes of God. Now we have to be concerned about Adam in our family, how he sees and hears us interact with each other.

Over the past five years, our son has taught me a lot about patience, learning from the mistakes that I made in the past with my daughter. Today, Adam is a ball of non-stop energy, talking, playing and wearing me out, especially during spring and Christmas break when he's not at school. My friend David Love, called me recently, asking, "Hi Jemal, how are you doing today?" When Adam's in school, I have a break, but when he's home all day long with me, it's hard.

David and I laughed when I said, "David, Adam is driving me crazy today. He keeps talking to me, daddy this and daddy that. Can we go do this, can we go play in the gym." Adam's like a little wind-up toy who just keeps going until he crashes asleep. My wife laughs and thinks that Adam is just a wee Jemal, always active and playing outside. Adam is not the kind of kid who has to take time to wake up before he's functioning, he's switched on from the moment he opens his eyes in the morning to the moment they close again at night flying around the house like a noisy hummingbird.

My son is a smart boy, learning to count, spell and read. I was driving recently, and Adam was looking out the window at the signs, saying, "Daddy, that sign says 50." I replied, "Adam, that's right, it's the speed limit," smiling back at him. Then he looks over at the speedometer and says, "Well daddy, how come you're going 70, the police are going to pull you over." When I park too close to a fire hydrant, Adam says, "Daddy, don't park too close or the policeman will take all the money out of your piggy bank." Being married and having Adam in our lives is challenging, but at the same time, it brings joy, happiness, and a grateful heart to God for His blessings.

What has helped our marriage the most is our faith and not bringing up the past when we disagree or have small arguments. We avoid leaving our problems for another day, we talk about it and solve the issue right away, as God wants us to do. Vincia appreciates that I have left my past behind, not talking about it with her unless she asks me to.

Before we were married, someone asked her if she was concerned that I might relapse one day. There are never any guarantees in life, but for Vincia, even the idea of me relapsing never entered her mind. I am so grateful and blessed that she respects me so much, never judging, and I respect her for the way she accepts me. We dedicate everything in our family and marriage to God who is the centre of our life.

We're raising our son under the spiritual guidance of the Holy Spirit, spending as much time as possible with him. This is very important to us, having him enrolled in a private, Christian school with principles that we adhere to in our spiritual, everyday walk of life. I want the best for my son, something that was not available for me when I was growing up as a boy. That's my hope, dreams and prayer for my son.

My wife takes to heart that we, as parents, must take and accept responsibility for Adam's spiritual growth and well-being. We don't care whether he becomes a garbage man or a brain surgeon, we care about and look forward to the day when Adam gives his life to Jesus. My wife and I don't have a five-year plan as many other couples do, we take each day as it arrives, praying for peace, inspiration, hope, and love in our family.

When I think back to why I wanted to get married again I was hesitant, not being able to fully escape the troubles of my previous marriages. I told my counsellor and myself that I was just going to live alone in my world. However, time does change one's thoughts and hopes. After spending many hours and months reading my bible and praying, I said to God and myself, "Ok, I'm going to give my hopes and thoughts about marriage a chance." It wasn't because I was not happy living alone … if I wanted to serve God, I needed to get married.

Paul tells us in 1 Corinthians 7:7-8: "I wish that all men were as I am. But each man has his gift from God; one has this gift, another has that. Now to the unmarried and the widows I say: It is good for them to stay unmarried, as I am." Paul says some have the gift of singleness and some the gift of marriage, and I didn't want temptation while living as a single man, so I chose marriage … God willing.

Some people do better as a team, serving God as a couple and a family. The most important thing in my life was not finding a mate and having children, but to seek God's direction, and to do this, I didn't want distractions in my life. Although I was happy living clean and sober, my life didn't feel fulfilled or complete … and today it does.

For Vincia, she was happy living single and alone. At times, there were thoughts about getting married, but she wasn't searching for someone. If she met someone who interested her, it would be good, she thought. She did tell me that, at times when she was in church or elsewhere, she looked around and thought, "Oh', I like that guy, oh' … I like that guy," but it wasn't something she allowed to distract her from her walk with God. She said, "Ok God, I'm not going to look, I trust you will bring the right person into my life because I'm going to choose the wrong person." She did stop looking but still had a desire in her heart to get married. "If I allow God to open the door, then He will keep it open for me," she said.

In many families today, both parents work to make ends meet, and for us, it can be difficult with Vincia working long, twelve-hour shifts as a nurse. Since Adam was born, notably when he was two years old, he started noticing that Vincia was gone. I could not console Adam when my wife left for work … he would cry and scream, probably thinking that his mom was leaving and not coming back. With her long shifts, sometimes Adam would only see her once every two days.

Love and Laughter

Once I started taking Adam with me to pick Vincia up at the Sky Train, Adam felt much better seeing that his mom was coming back home for the night. There were many adjustments, including me having to be aware of her tiredness after working her four-day, twelve-hour shifts at the hospital, taking her nearly two days to recover. I can see when she's tired, irritable, and I know when to keep my distance and not talk to her about some subjects.

Unlike how Vincia has to smile and be friendly to patients, her smile bucket is empty when she arrives home. She's so tired on multiple levels, from physical exhaustion to not sleeping enough, that she now has much more sympathy for me when I lay awake, unable to sleep. When I see and feel that Vincia is tired and quiet, I cook her meal … put it on the table, and say, "Bye." It may sound silly to some, but I've learned that for me to say more may be asking for trouble. I know for sure that if too much is said, we're most likely going to exchange unkind words to each other.

Since I began working only two days a week at UGM, our family life is much better. I could be working in higher, full-time positions as a supervisor and such, but my priorities are with my wife and son. To solve all these issues, we prayed and talked about it a lot and decided that working part-time was much better. Our marriage is far from perfect, and those who say theirs is are not being honest. We both laughed when Vincia said, "If they say their marriage is perfect, they're lying or there's something that one or both don't know what the other may be hiding."

We didn't go into our marriage blind about what to expect. Counselling helped us before getting married and attending a conference that talked about couples and families life after. Connection with other Christian couples, having Bible studies in our home and elsewhere, has helped ground us in our faith, knowing that God is in control. Other couples help us, we help them, and all of us learn how to be happier couples and better parents.

Sometimes the simple things in life still bring butterfly feelings into our marriage. Recently when Adam was in spring break camp, Vincia asked me to pick her up a cookie from Broadway Church. I thought, "What, I'm going to have to drive, park the car, and then drive the cookie to her work." I wouldn't do this for anyone else unless it's to pick up medicine for a sick friend. However, this was a delicious cookie, and I love to make her happy. When I stepped out of the hospital elevator, she was standing there smiling at me, not expecting me to come and deliver her cookie.

After I left the hospital, she texted me, "Jemal, you still look very handsome," and my response was, "Ya, I know, thank you." We still have fun playing and flirting with each other, having a sense of humour, which helps us both smile and laugh.

When we were at a three-day conference, before leaving our hotel room to go out for a romantic dinner, they told us to write a love letter to each other. Vincia's message to me was amazing. I still think about it today, smile, and feel deeply loved by my wife ... warmth in my heart that's hard to explain. I like this quote by Helen Keller ... it says what I feel, "The best and most beautiful things in the world cannot be seen or even touched. They must be felt with the heart." The words I read from my wife were incredibly touching, but even more so, were the messages I read between the lines, words of deep caring, emotion and tenderness.

Divine Direction

Vincia is much more of a talker than I am. When I'm tired after work in the evenings, it's difficult for me to listen when Vincia is speaking to me. Sometimes I think, "Oh, I wish we could talk about this tomorrow, not right now when I'm so tired." My mind is so full after listening to people all day long about their troubles that I'm exhausted when I get home.

But even though Vincia knows I'm tired, she continues, "Are you listening to me Jemal?" Of course, I answer, "Yes," but I'm not listening, only hearing her because my brain is still processing all that I heard and had to deal with at work. She sometimes does ramble on about her day but does hear and listen to what I say because it's important to her about what's important to me. Other times, we don't need to speak, we can tell what each other is thinking or what we say by our body language.

I can see when Vincia is tired, upset … it's not the right time to be near her or for a romantic moment, and she can tell when I'm not in the mood for talking. She used to meet me at the door when I arrived home after work and rambled on and on, like twenty miles an hour, but not now. Often, I would say, "Not now, I'm tired, just let me sit down and relax for a bit." I would sit down, watch some TV, and Vincia would wait for the right timing to approach me.

Today, my wife doesn't need to look at my face to see that I'm tired, she already knows without asking me … and I know the same with her. Being married for nine years we are blessed to have discernment, the perception of each other's wants and needs.

Even though we want to take care of situations right away, we have learned to be patient with each other rather than rush. This works out well because the wrong timing often results in adverse reactions and different responses. Vincia no longer meets me at the door after work. Marriage is learning the process of giving and taking with respect and love.

We'll be talking about something that needs an important decision, and I'll say, "Ok, let me think about it," and walk away. A few hours later, Vincia will walk over to me and say, "Well, have you thought about it yet, you have had three hours already." Usually, I have not decided yet and respond with, "No, I still need to think and pray about it, this is important to make the right choice … it isn't as simple as buying a dress; it's our new home."

Because Vincia has worked for so long as a nurse, she is used to making quick, crucial decisions on the fly, but there are procedures and policies to guide her decisions, which is not the case in our marriage. There are no rules and regulations to marriage. Before making important decisions, I take the matter to God. If I feel at peace with it, without stress, the right choice falls into place without any problems.

I know, without a doubt, that God has the right answers, the source of wisdom, He understands my past and future and protects my family in all that we do together. Proverbs 2:6-9 states, "For the Lord gives wisdom, and from his mouth come knowledge and understanding. Then you will understand what is right and just and fair, every good path." I simply ask as the Bible says, James 1:5, "If any of you lacks wisdom, he should ask God, who gives generously to all without finding fault, and it will be given to him." I know God wants to listen and talk to me, and as I pray, asking for His help, my decision will become clearer and firm. Proverbs 4:18 says, "The path of the righteous is like the first gleam of dawn, shining ever brighter till the full light of day."

When I sense anxiety or stress, I keep praying, asking God if my choice is right. James 3:15-17, "But the wisdom that comes from heaven is first of all pure; then peace-loving, considerate, submissive, full of mercy and good fruit, impartial and sincere." It helps me avoid being swayed by my emotions, unwise, selfish motives, or what others want me to do, things that I may not even be aware of.

Whatever decision I'm facing, there are biblical principles that help me make decisions, ones that are blessed by God. Even though Vincia sometimes wants an answer as soon as possible, she recognizes me being the head of our household, spiritually, and she appreciates the way I go to God for specific decisions … both of us learning to be patient with each other and our God. He is our master who gives us divine direction.

Spending Time – Keeping Our Marriage Together

Our special dating times didn't stop after we were married. When Vincia has finished her weekly shift, rested for a couple of days, and Adam is in school or daycare, we go out together on dates. Because of my wife's alternating work shifts, we don't plan a month ahead. We prepare the day before, and go out for breakfast, brunch and then see movies at the theatre. Watching a movie in the daytime is nice, it's not crowded, and we can relax and eat popcorn in romantic comfort. Other times we spend time with other couples at the movies, bowling, and Bible studies. Connecting with other couples, is essential to us, having fun, laughing and learning about each other.

Spending time together with other families, including our children, is even better now than when we first met and began dating. Everyone is smiling, having fun with the BBQ ... kind of, like what you would see on TV like the Waltons, only in the city.

Our Christian walk, dating life, and inter-family relationships helps give spiritual health to our marriage, reflecting on our walk with the Lord. Hebrews 10:24-25, "And let us consider how we may spur one another on toward love and good deeds, not giving up meeting together, as some are in the habit of doing, but encouraging one another ... and all the more as you see the Day approaching." Here is what we do, reaching out to other married couples with children, enjoying our times together, and encouraging each other.

Of course, there are times when things pop up that take me off course, especially if Vincia and I have been arguing about something, but we made vows before God. I think we've all been angry at a friend or spouse and don't even want to see them. My wife talked about this with me, saying, "We have to ask God to help us see people in a new light and give it over to God. Matthew 5:16, "Let your light shine before men in such a way that they may see your good works, and glorify your Father who is in heaven."

There are so many people in life that think about whether you're right or wrong, but it's not about that. In our marriage, we have to look at it as us being partners, and surround ourselves with people who want the best for our marriage. Avoiding people who give bad advice, we seek those who are honest and have our best interests at heart, and the truth in love always wins. Honesty with each other and friends is a big key to success. We look at our marriage as a legacy, an example to others in which we hope will inspire couples.

I strive to model Christian virtues of true spirituality, realizing that God has called my wife and me to be examples to others. Luke 6:40, "A disciple is not greater than his teacher, but everyone when fully trained will be like his teacher." As a Pastor, I have a responsibility to maintain a consistent example, found in the elements of spiritual character, in the character of Christ. Galatians 5:22, "But the fruit of the Spirit is love, joy, peace, forbearance, kindness, goodness, faithfulness."

Vincia and I have talked about how breaking our marriage apart would not only affect us, but how our neighbours and friends would look at it as well, probably thinking, "If those Christians can't make it, why should I or we even try?" Our children and relatives see it especially affecting our son. He could see it as, "Well, my parents didn't make it, so I'm not going to get married." And it has other far-reaching, ripple effects, like when a child sees their friend sad or stressed because he or her parents break up. So during the hard times, we try even harder to maintain unity.

If our marriage is not what it ought to be, others will not want to follow our example; they will turn away. If my Christian walk is contrary to what I say, it tells people that I am unreal or not following God's character. If I'm not following God's principles and Adam sees or hears me, I don't want to him to ask, "Daddy, if you can do and say that, why can't I?" My hope and prayers are that I am an example for him, speaking and doing things decently, with love, caring, compassion … influencing, and being a model for Adam to imitate.

I have a responsibility to be an image of reality, a proof that God forgives people, saves and changes lives, so that I can become a source of motivation for others, especially married couples struggling. 1 Thess. 1:6, "And you became imitators of us and of the Lord when you received the message with joy that comes from the Holy Spirit, despite great affliction."

Reading these Bible passages and praying helps me to understand, keeping our marriage healthy. 2 Cor. 4:15-18, "For all these things are for your sake, so that the grace that is including more and more people may cause thanksgiving to increase to the glory of God. Therefore, we do not despair, but even if our physical body is wearing away, our inner person is being renewed day by day. For our momentary, light suffering is producing for us an eternal weight of glory far beyond all comparison because we are not looking at what can be seen, but at what cannot be seen. For what can be seen is temporary, but what cannot be seen is eternal." I preached about this at the Broadway Church recently, about believing without seeing.

My marriage is so important to me, that through faith and believing in Christ, I know that He is the master, and deserves all the glory in our marriage and family life. When Christ returns, I will stand before him in awe, not ashamed. 1 John 2:28, "And now, dear children, continue in him, so that when he appears, we may be confident and unashamed before him at his coming."

Marriage and Money

Vincia works hard long hours as a nurse at a Vancouver hospital, and has an income above what I earn as an outreach worker and pastor. After we were married, I wanted to catch up to her income. I suppose it's just a 'man-thing' where the husband thinks he should, or usually does, bring home more money than his wife. We talked about it for quite some time before realizing that it's just money and it's God's money anyway, not ours.

So, we put it all together, remembering what Mathew said, "Seek first the kingdom of God and his righteousness, and all these things will be added to you," Matthew 6:33. We both know that surviving the "for richer, for poorer" part of our vows begins with understanding that God has a plan for us about our finances. Rather than seeing the goal of our marriage as the accumulation of things, we seek that which builds a secure relationship, putting God first in our lives. We talk and pray about our goals and objectives, avoiding financial bondage to things we want, rather than what we need. We invite God into our finances, and He does amazing things, especially if we ask Him to enter into the process. I ask God to guide me in how He wants me to earn an income, and how to use it.

We may not have all we want, but we do have all we need. Philippians 4:19, "And my God will supply every need of yours according to his riches in glory in Christ Jesus." If I keep looking to what personal things I want for myself or my family, I tend not to look to God ... I've taken back control over my life. My past life was all about me wanting and striving to be in control, and that didn't work out well, it almost killed me. "Many are the plans in the mind of a man, but it is the purpose of the Lord that will stand," Proverbs 19:21. My wife and I try not to be concerned or worry about our marriage and finances, "Therefore do not be anxious about tomorrow, for tomorrow will be anxious for itself. Sufficient for the day is its own trouble," Matthew 6:34.

Chapter 15

Shared Wisdom

"If any of you lacks wisdom, let him ask of God, who gives to all liberally and without reproach, and it will be given to him." - James 1:5 (NKJV)

This wisdom is not mine, but it is what God has taught me; I have made him my guide. Therefore, I must tell you first that this is what I have learned after falling in life. I give Him credit for picking me up and continuing to teach me.

The following, are questions that my wife has asked me that she thinks are important for people on this journey.

Describe your spiritual walk today?

I am far from being the spiritually mature person that I should or want to be, but I am trying each day to grow closer to God. It is important to God to see us trying each day. 1 Samuel 15:22: "Has the Lord as great delight in burnt offerings and sacrifices, as in obeying the voice of the Lord? Behold, to obey is better than sacrifice, And to heed than the fat of rams." Just as we want to see our children grow physically, God desires that we grow in our walk and not stay in the same place.

One way to test this is to compare your walk each month or year. Am I a more mature person today as compared to last year? 1Corinthians 3:2, "I fed you with milk and not with solid food; for until now you were not able to receive it, and even now you are still not able."

If not, I need to see what's in my life that needs changing. Maturity takes time and sacrifice. Each day, I devote myself to prayer, taking time to read and meditate on His word; surrounding myself with mature men of God who mentor and speak in my life.

The internet has too much false information from fools that will lead you astray, so I ask God for wisdom to sift them out. Listening to my favourite preacher and music when I am alone at home fills my empty moments, much different for me today as compared to my previous life. These times energize me with spiritual food because His word and praise are in the songs.

What advice do you have for people still stuck in addiction?

I have learned never to stop asking questions and never stop reaching out for help. One day you will beat this addiction and change your life; your addiction is not your identity, you are worth so much more. I know what it's like because, for many years, I viewed my existence as something else, sometimes feeling worthless or unfixable. The wrong ways I defined myself arose naturally in my heart and mind; false identities which others and I saw or thought. That is untrue and not who I was, and neither is it the real you.

You must never give up, but keep looking up and holding onto hope that one day you too will be telling your story and it will be inspiring to others. Never feed yourself the lie that you are damaged, or you are too far-gone that no one can help you. I failed in my search for fulfillment in relationships, jobs, money, achievements, possessions and a hundred other things. My sense of self was based on having lots of money, on performance, and on the approval of others. For too long, I let character defects and sins define me: an angry man, an addict, an anxious person. But there is another identity, a core identity.

God is with you in that dark alley, and he can walk with you as you go towards the light. Addiction is a lonely and shadowy road of suffering. However, never forget that God is right beside you and calling you to come to him. He is the only one who can get you out and keep you out. Ignore the awful words that society and even family members will use to describe you and your addiction. I discovered that by listening to what others were say or from looking inside myself, hearing the voices from my internal dialogue saying I was unworthy or not enough, was false.

Choose to listen to anyone who lifts you up and helps you feel good about yourself. Proverbs 12:18, "There is one who speaks like the piercings of a sword, But the tongue of the wise promotes health." Resist shame and guilt because these will pull you deeper into the darkness. Instead, wrap yourself in the love of God until you have the strength to ask for help, which will pull you away from the hold your addiction has on you. John 10:10, "The thief does not come except to steal, and to kill, and to destroy. I have come that they may have life and that they may have it more abundantly."

How do you get your sexual addiction under control on a daily basis?

In the Psalms 51:4, David cries out to God, "Against you and you alone have I sinned. Against You, You only, have I sinned, And done this evil in Your sight—That You may be found just when You speak, And blameless when You judge." The key to conquering any addiction is realizing that it is against God first. We hurt our wives and sisters in Christ, but we need to be honest and know that this is a sin against a holy God.

2 Timothy 1:9 (NKJV), "Who has saved us and called us with a holy calling, not according to our works, but according to His own purpose and grace which was given to us in Christ Jesus before time began."

Often, I am surrounded by images of half-dressed women on a daily basis. I do not wait for women to cover themselves as a way to solve this problem because it will never happen. We live in a fallen world. Job 31:1, "I have made a covenant with my eyes." Today when I see a woman or an image that would bring back memories, I quickly look away and quietly say verses that I have memorized. You cannot fight this battle unprepared. You need to use God's word, it is powerful, and it works. Being unprepared can be fatal and pull oneself down into darkness.

Sometimes, just standing in the bank and seeing a woman exposing her chest can trigger a memory. However, I quickly look away and speak God's word under my breath. This sin is hard, but it is not that hard when you fight with God at your side.

Proverb 6:27 says, "Can a man take fire to his bosom, and his clothes not be burned?" This is a hidden addiction, but all secrets eventually come to the surface. Ultimately, this secret will burn you and all the people around you. It will destroy your opportunity to witness to others if you do not deal with it.

I also made a promise to myself never to be alone with another woman. Even if it's the wife of a friend; if my wife cannot be there, I will meet her another time. My wife did not know about this addiction that I struggled with until writing this book, and she always wondered why I lived my life that way.

"Oh just go, I know you are not cheating on me" she would say. I told her I choose to live my life this way because I wanted to respect her and I didn't want for someone to say that I am meeting a woman by myself who is not my wife. This is something that God impressed on my heart after He brought me out of my sexual addiction. It is about respecting and protecting women. My job is to protect Vincia and our marriage.

About three and a half years ago, Vincia came to me with something that God had put in her heart. She said that she felt that God was telling her to change how she dressed. I asked her, "What's wrong with how you dress?" She said that she was looking into dressing more modestly. Believe me, my wife was not wearing booty shorts or anything else inappropriate. However, I was not going to get in the way if God was leading her down a path. I told her that I would pray for her obedience. She believed that God wanted her to stop wearing pants and she had a hard time because she loved wearing jeans. But once she came to this decision, there was no stopping her.

She felt that her body was for me only and that pants exposed curves of her body too much. I respect her for making this decision as she has endured many negative comments because of it. Me personally, I like how she dresses now as it reminds me of how I grew up. It surprised me when she made this decision, but I believe that God took her down this path. While writing this book it has brought us closer as we talked about sexuality and the power of visual suggestions.

Do what God commanded to do, run and flee from sexual addiction. 1 Corinthians 6:18, "Flee sexual immorality. Every sin that a man does is outside the body, but he who commits sexual immorality sins against his own body."

What has marriage taught you?

I was determined to make this marriage work but I had no foundation or wisdom to base it on given that my previous two marriages failed; so this time I put God in the centre. He helped me to make proper decisions and to love Vincia as He commanded me to. He has shown me how to love her even when I am angry or when I am tired. Marriage has taught me how to be selfless and to put the needs of others first. Addiction wants you to think about yourself first and not care about how it will hurt the people around you.

I learned the real power of prayer; spending time in God's words changed my life. He has given me wisdom about situations to make decisions to protect my family, teaching me to love during the difficult times when the enemy whispers to me that running would be easier.

Life and God have taught about the small things that women appreciate. Vincia doesn't want or need expensive gifts anymore. She wants and desires practical gifts. On her last birthday, I did something just as a favour to her, and she made such a big deal about it. She worked the day before her birthday and had the next day off. A basket full of laundry needed washing and Vincia usually does it. But it was her birthday, and off to work the next day, so I did the laundry for her and had the clothes folded on the bed when she came home. It may not seem romantic to some, but it was something that freed up her birthday so that she could enjoy it and not have to worry about household stuff. Yes, I cook, but I don't do laundry, and dislike it, but I did it that time as a way to show my love practically.

What advice would you give to men trying to choose a wife?

I asked God to bring someone into my life that wanted the same things spiritually that I wanted. Knowing that rarely are two people at the same place spiritually, I wanted someone to be walking and hungry for God. I didn't want a marriage where I would have to drag my wife to church. I left my hopes in God's hands; where only He can know for sure that a person is truly spiritual. Some people look like they are walking a holy life, but many are chameleons.

Before going for coffee or dating Vincia, I asked God to show me if Vincia was the right person for me. I sought guidance from trusted, wise friends, and asked people to pray for me. I continued to pray, seeking His will, Galatians 1:16, "I did not immediately confer with flesh and blood." I did ask a few friends for guidance, but I began with God as the primary one before I asked others; because only He knows who she genuinely is.

One night a friend and I went out partying at a club in Portland, Oregon. I saw a black girl who looked beautiful, hair well done, wearing an attractive, tight outfit. I went over to talk to her and we ended up drinking together before ending up at my place. I woke up the next morning next to her but things had changed. When I looked over at her, I wondered who she was. I got up and went to the bathroom, thinking I was so drunk last night that I ended up in the wrong room.

"So who was in my bed," I thought. I went back out and woke her up. "Who are you and what are you doing in my bed?" She told me that I brought her home last night. "Not you, I brought home a different woman." She then went into the bathroom and came out as the woman I remembered in the club. I told her that I had no idea she was a store-bought woman. We started to argue, we fought and then she left. This is a funny story, but many men choose their wife only based on how they look. Let God help you and reveal if this woman is for you.

What helped me the most, was being patient, not rushing as soon as I met Vincia. Just spending time with her and with God was all I wanted for a while. He showed me not just to fall in love with my eyes, but to look deeper and see what she stands for and what she believes.

How do family members deal with a loved one who is struggling with an addiction?

Love is all-powerful; something that often is invisible to addicts. They don't feel loved, cared about, nor do they trust. Letting a loved one know you care about and love them is essential; and that what you are going to do is hard but necessary. Too many family members will not let their loved ones fall and pick themselves up. Family members keep carrying them and enabling them by giving them money. Supporting their addiction to keep them close to you will not help them in the long run, as they feel no compulsion or need to seek help on their own.

Addicts must see their addiction for what it is, they need to hate addiction and see how it's destroying them. For me, I had to lose everything and be at the end of my rope. I learned the hard way that my addiction robbed me like a thief in the night.

That is a hard thing to do, but it must be accomplished for recovery to be successful. They must hate where they are and have hope for where they want to be, and the life they want to have. An addicted family member might hate you for cutting them off financially, but they will eventually thank you one day for taking this vital step that saved their life.

What advice would you give to someone to help them stay clean and sober for the rest of their life?

Ephesian 1:4-6, "Just as He chose us in Him before the foundation of the world, that we should be holy and without blame before Him in love, having predestined us to adoption as sons by Jesus Christ to Himself, according to the good pleasure of His will, to the praise of the glory of His grace, by which He made us accepted in the Beloved." Never forget that God is the only one that is going make this process successful. Surrender your life to Him and His plan for your life.

I set goals for my life that are reasonable but not too many at a time. I made a promise to myself that for one year after recovery I would not date anyone. I knew that whatever goal I set, the enemy was going to seek a way to trip me up. I finished the program in May, and I met Vincia in September. The enemy tried to tell me that I did not have to wait a year to ask her out and that it would not matter if I broke this promise. First, I remained strong in my faith and recovery, sticking to my goal that made me stronger. Recovery is hard; each day filled with battles and victories, the latter carrying me forward in faith.

I knew what my triggers were and stayed away from them. For the first few years, I didn't enter a place with the smell of alcohol. I can go there now, but in the early stages, the smell brought back too many memories. I had to get new friends and sometimes say no to invitations; setting boundaries to keep me safe. Some people didn't understand why I refused to go to certain places, but I had to be responsible and say, "No." I surrounded myself with people who wanted me to succeed, being honest with them about my past, and how I was feeling. I didn't dwell on my past mistakes but remembered it to stay clean and remain humble.

I am chosen, adopted, redeemed, forgiven, and unconditionally loved and accepted with the hope of spending eternity with God. My love and core identity are in Christ, never altered by what I do or by what others think and say; thus, as I have faith and trust in Him, I am free to spread His Gospel. I know who I am, and I am grateful and blessed beyond words. Remaining in Christ involves attuning my ear to God's voice, which continues to say, "You are my own dear Son. I am pleased with you."

I was forced to walk a difficult and painful road. But what I discovered is that God was always beside me calling me to walk the path that He had chosen for me. I know this is the truth and that He is doing the same for you too.

Joel 2:25-27

"So I will restore to you the years that the swarming locust has eaten, The crawling locust, The consuming locust, And the chewing locust, My great army which I sent among you. You shall eat in plenty and be satisfied, And praise the name of the Lord your God, Who has dealt wondrously with you; And My people shall never be put to shame. Then you shall know that I am in the midst of Israel: I am the Lord your God And there is no other. My people shall never be put to shame"

BOOK REVIEWS

Pastor Darin Latham: I have lived a relatively active life. I've travelled the world and been placed in some unusual situations over the years. I thought that I had my fair share of stories to tell of being placed in "tight spots" and facing "challenging moments," stories I could pull out and share in the course of a conversation.

Then I met Jemal... His life has been a series of "tight spots" and "challenging moments" that are beyond what most of us could ever imagine. But it's not so much what happened "to" him that makes Jemal's life stand out. It is what happened "in" him...
It's been said that, "wisdom does not come from the circumstances in your life, wisdom comes from how you ultimately respond to the circumstances in your life." If that is true, you are about to read the story of a very wise man.

Over the years, I have watched Jemal transition from a single man to a married man. I have watched him transform into a loving husband and then doting father. I have watched him live out a calling to reach men and women who find themselves at the very bottom of the social ladder: men and women who are stuck; men and women who wander the streets of our city. I used to wonder what fueled Jemal's drive to head into that battleground - day after day, night after night. After reading his story, I no longer wonder.

Dr. Robert N. Thompson, Manager, UGM: Jemal Damtawe shares his incredible life story of being enslaved as a child-soldier in Ethiopia, being a stow-away on a tanker taking him around the world, to a life of addiction on Vancouver's Downtown Eastside to encountering Jesus in a skid row recuse mission where he now serves as an Outreach Worker serving the "least of these". Jemal not only shares of his years of addiction but also his new found life as a husband, father, friend, Outreach Worker and Pastor.

I have had the honor and privilege of working alongside Jemal, attending his wedding and witnessing the joy restored after years of seeing what the 'locusts have eaten". Jemal's story is a blessing to anyone who will take the time to read it. Enjoy the ride.

Jeremiah Touchbourne: A childhood spent surviving a civil war in Africa. An adulthood spent enslaved to alcohol, drugs and gangs in North America. Jemal's story of salvation is one of God's greatest modern day miracles. Pastor Jemal will inspire you and give you hope to believe that with Jesus Christ all people can be saved.

Curt Bruneski: Jemal leads us on a journey from gut-wrenching sorrow, to overwhelming relief and joy. His open and candid sharing of his life experiences are at times difficult to hear and comprehend, and yet, helps us to see and understand how amazing God's ability to redeem us truly is. God's love is unfailing, even in the darkest moments of our lives. What a wonderful story of redemption and victory.

Pastor Fari Maghami: I am excited to commend Jemal Damtawe's book to you. Having known Jemal since 2008 as a dear friend, and worked together as outreach workers at the Union Gospel Mission in Downtown Eastside Vancouver, I know his faith is genuine and his transformation credible. His life has been filled with heart-wrenching experiences, but also with countless fascinating and courageous stories of triumph. His journey through and out of war, addiction and crime will touch your heart and inspire you to believe that Christ can reach anyone in any circumstance.

Peter Steffens: I am not alone; the book guides me to overcome my fears, trusting God to a higher level, and about the power of forgiveness. Jemal's honesty and faithfulness helped me realize the truth in scripture: "You shall know the truth, and the truth shall set you free." John 8:32.

Author: Jemal Damtawe
Cover design: Jason van Dyk
Guest Editor: Angela Paterson
Introduction: Vincia Damtawe
Interviewer/Transcribing: David E Love
Prologue: Pastor Darin Latham

---

[i] Courage to Come Back (https://couragetocomeback.ca)

Made in the USA
Columbia, SC
10 August 2018